ALIFA RIFAAT is Egyptian and has spent all her life in the Arab world, immersed in the traditions and culture of Islam. She was brought up in Egypt, a devout Muslim, strictly adhering to the Islamic way of life and well versed in the Qur'an and religious teachings. Her education and a possible future career in art were curtailed when she married – her parents' alternative to university. A widow, she now lives in Cairo with her three children.

Largely divorced from Western influences, speaking and writing only Arabic, Alifa Rifaat allows the reader a rare and enlightening glimpse of women's conditions in a male-dominated environment. Her originality lies not in any overt and conventional feminist approach, but rather through her implicit criticisms of the male neglect of Islamic obligations to women, particularly in family life and marital relationships. She challenges behaviour from within the accepted framework of her society's religion and laws.

Distant View of a Minaret was first published in English in 1983, by Quartet Books. Two of the stories have been broadcast on BBC Radio 3.

DENYS JOHNSON-DAVIES, the much-praised translator of these stories, is a distinguished Arabist. His involvement with Arab culture has spanned many years, and in his varied career he has lived in the Gulf, Beirut and Cairo, working as a lecturer in English literature and Arabic translation, an oil company representative, a lawyer, businessman and head of an Arabic radio station.

ALIFA RIFAAT

DISTANT VIEW
OF A MINARET

AND OTHER STORIES

Selected and translated from the Arabic by
Denys Johnson-Davies

HEINEMANN

Heinemann Educational Publishers
Halley Court, Jordan Hill, Oxford OX2 8EJ
A part of Harcourt Education Limited

Heinemann: A Division of Reed Publishing (USA) Inc.
361 Hanover Street, Portsmouth, NH 03801-3912, USA

Heinemann Publishers (Pty) Limited
PO Box 781940, Sandton 2146, Johannesburg, South Africa

OXFORD   MELBOURNE   AUCKLAND
JOHANNESBURG   KUALA LUMPUR   GABORONE
PORTSMOUTH (NH) USA   CHICAGO

First published by Quartet Books Ltd 1983
First published by Heinemann Educational Books Ltd
in the African Writers Series as AWS 271
and the Arab Authors as AA 23 in 1985
First published in this edition, 1987

British Library Cataloguing in Publication Data
Rifaat, Alifa
Distant view of a minaret: and other stories. – African writers series.
I. Title   II. Johnson-Davies, Denys   III. Series
892'.7236[F]   PJ7860.13/

ISBN 0-435-90912-6

Printed and bound in Great Britain by
Cox & Wyman Ltd, Reading, Berkshire

03   04   15   14   13

CONTENTS

Translator's Foreword

More convincingly than any other woman writing in Arabic today, Alifa Rifaat, an Egyptian in her early fifties, lifts the veil on what it means to be a woman living within a traditional Muslim society. Restricting herself in the main to the short story, her writing has progressed over the years from an early romanticism, often marred by sentimentality, to a more recent sparse realism. Without the benefit of a university education – the expression of a desire to continue her education and to study art was interpreted by her family as a sign that it was time to find her a suitable husband – she possesses no competence in a foreign language. Her reading has thus been restricted to Arab writers of fiction and such foreign fiction as has been translated into Arabic; in addition she is deeply read in works of religion, in particular the Qur'an and the Hadith (the Sayings of the Prophet). Most of her married life has been spent in various parts of provincial Egypt, which provide the settings for many of her stories; apart from this her only travels outside Cairo have been two recent visits to Mecca and Medina for the purpose of performing the Pilgrimage. At first consideration this would appear an unpromising background for a writer of fiction; yet it is these very limitations that have imposed upon her writing its freshness and actuality.

Most of her stories express, implicitly rather than explicitly, a revolt against many of the norms and attitudes, particularly those related to woman and her place in society. Her revolt, despite the frank terms in which it is expressed, remains within a strictly religious, even orthodox, framework. In this she differs wholly from the women writers of Beirut – a movement that began with Leila Baalbaki and is carried on by such writers as Ghada Samman and Hanan Shaykh – whose Arab form of women's lib. is inspired by its Western counterpart. Alifa Rifaat's revolt falls far short of suggesting that there be any change in the traditional role of women in a Muslim society, and the last place she would look for inspiration for any change would be the Christian West.

While Alifa Rifaat would not of course disagree with the Qur'anic precept that 'men are in charge of women', she would appear to take the view that this automatically places upon men the burden of behaving towards women with kindness and generosity – as is enjoined by the Qur'an. If a man's behaviour falls short of what is expected of him, the woman's natural acceptance of her role is likely to change to contempt and rebellion. Alifa Rifaat's revolt, therefore, is merely against certain man-made interpretations and accretions that have grown up over the years and remain unquestioned by the majority of both men and women.

Two subjects predominate in her stories: sex and death. In such stories as 'The Long Night of Winter', 'Distant View of a Minaret' and 'Bahiyya's Eyes', woman's wish (and right) to be sexually fulfilled is openly stated. The directness with which these stories are handled, even the fact that she deals with sexual themes and suggests that women can have views and rights in these matters, is unusual in such a society. Nevertheless, for all the frankness in her treatment of sex, Alifa Rifaat's point of view is radically different from any postured by Western women's lib. Love and sex outside the boundaries of marriage is no part of the scenery of her stories. For her there is nothing romantic about adultery: it is, quite simply, a sin. While many of her stories deal with sexual frustration, she posits no easy solution; certainly it does not lie in a change of partner. It is part of a woman's role in life to see that a marriage, whether successful or not from her standpoint, continues.

In 'My World of the Unknown', a story written several years before the others in this collection, the woman's fantasies as she lies beside her unloving and unloved husband are not of possible bliss in the arms of a more adequate man but of a dreamworld that is obviously, though perhaps not consciously, Freudian.

The mental landscape within which Alifa Rifaat works is one that is unfamiliar to most Western readers. It is essentially a religious one: the *muezzin's* call to prayer and the five daily prayers are an integral part of the lives of most of her characters, be they peasants or members of the middle class. In 'Distant View of a Minaret' the prayers are described as being like punctuation marks that give daily life its meaning. Islam is a religion whose particular dye colours each hour of each day, every act and word. Stemming from this religious backcloth is the writer's preoccupation with death: its inevitability and finality, also its sheer ordinariness. In religious terms life is merely a preparation for death, and the life of this world – as the Qur'an tells us repeatedly – is but 'a sport and a pastime'. The West's attitude to death can be seen from the way in which the traditional folktale ends with the main character triumphing and 'living happily ever after'; the Muslim storyteller, on the other hand, feels obliged to remind us that while the hero may come through his adventures safely he will only live on happily 'until the Destroyer of Worldly Pleasures comes to him'. In Alifa Rifaat's stories death is seldom far away.

In dealing with such universal themes as sex and death the writer does so within the confines of her own particular culture and set of moral values. Such though is the directness and sincerity of the writing that these stories rise above their local context and are placed within the emotional reach of any reader willing to enter this unfamiliar territory.

Denys Johnson-Davies, 1983

Distant View of a Minaret

୰୰୰୰୰୰୰୰୰୰୰୰୰୰୰୰୰୰୰୰୰୰୰୰୰୰

Through half-closed eyes she looked at her husband. Lying on his right side, his body was intertwined with hers and his head bent over her right shoulder. As usual at such times she felt that he inhabited a world utterly different from hers, a world from which she had been excluded. Only half-aware of the movements of his body, she turned her head to one side and stared up at the ceiling, where she noticed a spider's web. She told herself she'd have to get out the long broom and brush it down.

When they were first married she had tried to will her husband into sensing the desire that burned within her and so continuing the act longer; she had been too shy and conscious of the conventions to express such wishes openly. Later on, feeling herself sometimes to be on the brink of the experience some of her married women friends talked of in hushed terms, she had found the courage to be explicit about what she wanted. At such moments it had seemed to her that all she needed was just one more movement and her body and soul would be quenched, that once achieved they would between them know how to repeat the experience. But on each occasion, when breathlessly imploring him to continue, he would – as though purposely to deprive her – quicken his movements and bring the act to an abrupt end. Sometimes she had tried in vain to maintain the rhythmic movements a little longer, but always he would stop her. The last time she had made such an attempt, so desperate was she at this critical moment, that she had dug her fingernails into his back, compelling him to remain inside her. He had given a shout as he pushed her away and slipped from her:

'Are you mad, woman? Do you want to kill me?'

It was as though he had made an indelible tattoo mark of shame deep inside her, so that whenever she thought of the incident she felt a flush coming to her face. Thenceforth she had submitted to her passive role, sometimes asking herself: 'Perhaps it's me who's at fault. Perhaps I'm unreasonable in my demands and don't know how to react to him properly.'

There had been occasions when he had indicated that he had had relationships with other women, and sometimes she had suspicions that maybe he still had affairs, and she was surprised that the idea no longer upset her.

She was suddenly aroused from her thoughts by his more urgent movements. She turned to him and watched him struggling in the world he occupied on his own. His eyes were tight closed, his lips drawn down in an ugly contortion, and the veins in his neck stood out. She felt his hand on her leg, seizing it above the knee and thrusting it sideways as his movements became more frenzied. She stared up at her foot that now pointed towards the spider's web and noted her toenails needed cutting.

As often happened at this moment she heard the call to afternoon prayers filtering through the shutters of the closed window and bringing her back to reality. With a groan he let go of her thigh and immediately withdrew. He took a small towel from under the pillow, wrapped it round himself, turned his back to her and went to sleep.

She rose and hobbled to the bathroom where she seated herself on the bidet and washed herself. No longer did she feel any desire to complete the act with herself as she used to do in the first years of marriage. Under the shower she gave her right side to the warm water, then her left, repeating the formula of faith as the water coursed down her body.[1] She wrapped her soaking hair in a towel and wound a large second one under her armpits. Returning to the

2

bedroom, she put on a long house-gown, then took up the prayer carpet from on top of the wardrobe and shut the door behind her.

As she passed through the living room, the sounds of pop music came to her from the room of her son Mahmoud. She smiled as she imagined him stretched out on his bed, a school book held in front of him; she was amazed at his ability to concentrate in the face of such noise. She closed the living room door, spread the rug and began her prayers. When she had performed the four *rak'as*[2] she seated herself on the edge of the prayer carpet and counted off her glorifications of the Almighty, three at a time on the joints of each finger. It was late autumn and the time for the sunset prayer would soon come and she enjoyed the thought that she would soon be praying again. Her five daily prayers were like punctuation marks that divided up and gave meaning to her life. Each prayer had for her a distinct quality, just as different foods had their own flavours. She folded up the carpet and went out onto the small balcony.

Dusting off the cane chair that stood there, she seated herself and looked down at the street from the sixth floor. She was assailed by the din of buses, the hooting of cars, the cries of street vendors and the raucous noise of competing radios from nearby flats. Clouds of smoke rose up from the outpourings of car exhausts veiling the view of the tall solitary minaret that could be seen between two towering blocks of flats. This single minaret, one of the twin minarets of the Mosque of Sultan Hasan, with above it a thin slice of the Citadel, was all that was now left of the panoramic view she had once had of old Cairo, with its countless mosques and minarets against a background of the Mokattam Hills and Mohamed Ali's Citadel.

Before marriage she had dreamed of having a house with a small garden in a quiet suburb such as Maadi or Helwan. On finding that it would be a long journey for her husband to his work in the centre of the city, she had settled for this flat because of its view. But with the passing of the years, buildings had risen on all sides, gradually narrowing the view. In time this single minaret would also be obscured by some new building.

Aware of the approach of the call to sunset prayers, she left the balcony and went to the kitchen to prepare her husband's coffee. She filled the brass *kanaka*[3] with water and added a spoonful of coffee and a spoonful of sugar. Just as it was about to boil over she removed it from the stove and placed it on the tray with the coffee cup, for he liked to have the coffee poured out in front of him. She expected to find him sitting up in bed smoking a cigarette. The strange way his body was twisted immediately told her that something was wrong. She approached the bed and looked into the eyes that stared into space and suddenly she was aware of the odour of death in the room. She left and placed the tray in the living room before passing through to her son's room. He looked up as she entered and immediately switched off the radio and stood up:

'What's wrong, mother?'

'It's your father . . .'

'He's had another attack?'

She nodded. 'Go downstairs to the neighbours and ring Dr Ramzi. Ask him to come right away.'

She returned to the living room and poured out the coffee for herself. She was surprised at how calm she was.

Notes

1. Islam demands that after intercourse the whole body be washed.
2. The various movements of bending and prostration that make up the set prayer in Islam. The number of *rak'as* differ according to which of the five daily prayers is being performed.
3. The special pot in which Turkish coffee is prepared.

Bahiyya's Eyes[1]

~~~~~~

We praise Him and thank Him for His favour for whatever He decides. Here I am, daughter, alive and well, still like a cat with seven lives. Forgive me if I worried you by getting our neighbour to write you a letter asking you to come and stay with me for a while so that my eyes could take their fill of you. You see, a few days ago I decided to take myself off to the government hospital. I washed my *galabia* and my head-veil overnight so I'd be nice and clean for the doctor. I got fed up telling people to take me to the doctor's whenever someone passed by me. They kept saying to me: 'Ma, just wait till we find you a donkey to take you there – it's too far for you.' And then they'd just put it out of their minds. Anyway, that's life for you, and everyone's got his excuse. So, I'm telling you, I got myself up early and put on my *galabia* which still wasn't all that dry except I told myself it would dry out on the way. I took up the palm branch stick I use for chasing up my chickens and put myself into Allah's hands. Off I walked and eventually I got there. The nurse, Allah keep her safe, said to me: 'Mother, support yourself on my arm and never mind that stick of yours,' and straight away she took me in to see the doctor. Directly he saw me he said: 'Bahiyya, sit down on the chair in front of me.' I said to him: 'Your Honour, excuse me but it wouldn't be right – can the eye rise higher than the eyebrow?' He laughed and said: 'Sit down, Bahiyya, so I can examine you.' So, my dear, I sat myself down and he put on an electric light and with his own hand he took off my

5

head-veil and went on peering for a while into one eye and then into the other, while I was so embarrassed I didn't know what to say. Then he asked me: 'Tell me, Bahiyya, about your eyes and what you feel.' So I said to him: 'May the Lord light your path and protect your sight, my eyes used to be beautiful and round as saucers and I used to be able to spot someone walking as far away as the other side of the canal and be able to tell you who it was.' He said to me: 'These eyes of yours must have been troubling you for a long time. Can you tell me when they first started hurting you?' I said to him: 'May the good Lord never bring you any harm, sir, I'm a poor woman and all on my own, you see my husband died long ago and left me with the children to bring up as best I could and all I could think about is how I'd get tomorrow's bread. By the precious life of Your Honour, I can't remember when they first started closing up and filling with stuff. After a little while they'd get better and I'd put kohl on them and they'd be fine. But a couple of years ago I found the light draining out of them bit by bit like water from a cracked pitcher. I told myself I was getting old – and old age holds its warnings. But for some time now I've been finding tears flowing from them, you'd think it was rain. So I told myself it was high time I went to be examined by the doctor – our Lord is forgiving and merciful.' Then, daughter, he told me I'd made a big mistake and that I should have gone to him ages ago, and that it was all caused by the flies and the dirt. Anyway, he wrote me out a piece of paper and told me it was for some drops that would do me good. You ask me how often I use them? I tell you I didn't even trouble to get them though they told me they were for free. No, my child, I know and the doctor knows that there's no hospital has any drops that will bring back my sight. As I left I said to the nurse: 'Dear, hand me the stick 'cos it seems I'll be holding it all the time from now on.' Bless them, they did what they could, but cure lies in the hands of Allah alone. Daughter, it's all written on the forehead and there's not a doctor alive or dead can change fate. And what was all that he was saying about flies? Perhaps in his books they tell him it's from flies, but I know better. It all comes from the tears I shed since my mother first bore me and they held me up by the leg and found I was a girl. The whole of my life I went on crying and how often my mother'd tell me not to but it wasn't any use. My mother, Allah have mercy on her, was good and kind to us, she'd take us one by one every night and wash our faces and put us down to sleep alongside each other on the bench above the stove, while she, Awwad and my father'd sleep to one side. Three of us girls and a boy were the ones that lived: your Uncle Awwad was the one I came directly after – he was just ahead of me – and then there was your Aunt Nazeera and your Aunt Fadeela, Allah have mercy on her. Daughter, it's all a question of fate and destiny and it's that that made me write to you and ask you to come right away so I could take a good long look at you before my sight goes and I'm not able to tell white from black. My mother was always saying about me that I took things too much to heart as though I was always looking for something to cry about. And what good did it do me except that I ruined my eyes? My poor sister Fadeela had more reason to cry than me. How she suffered and didn't see a day's happiness in her life! When the bit of glass got into her foot and it swelled up, she went on screaming with the pain day and night, poor thing, before she died and she was still only a child. After she died I and your Aunt Nazeera were left, also your Uncle Awwad. As he grew up he became worse and worse with us, always pinching us and hitting us. It was as if he enjoyed hearing us scream. When we complained to my mother, Allah have mercy upon her, she'd tell us 'When your father's gone he'll be the man in the family and what he says goes so you'd better get used to it.' Whenever she used to go off to the field with my father she'd always take Awwad along with them and she'd lock up us girls at home. When we grew up a bit they'd get us to go out in the lanes to collect up the dung for my mother to sell as fuel to the man who owned the bakery. Nazeera and I would each make a heap of cowpats on the roof and mine was always more than twice as large as hers. The fact is I was clever and bright and full of energy. I was also the best looking of us sisters and so the evil eye was on me.

While we were spending the whole day collecting up the dung, Awwad would be playing in the water channel or romping round the fields, and when he came home he'd expect us to serve him like my mother served my father. He'd just sit back and think up things for us to do and find fault with us so he could give us a clout over the ear. Of course our life was the same as that of all the other girls, but it seems they were able to take it and not care a hang and just laugh it off. But my nature wasn't the same and the tears were always running down my cheeks. It was like my eyes were preparing themselves for what was to come, because it's not as if life got any easier as I grew up. Just the opposite. The fact is there's no joy for a girl in growing up, it's just one disaster after another till you end up an old woman who's good for nothing and who's real lucky if she finds someone to feel sorry for her. No, daughter, don't say it's not so. You tell me, then, what use I am. It's not every daughter who's kind enough to trail all the way from the town to our village just to visit her mother, Allah bless you through the glory of the Prophet. I'm sorry, daughter, if I've not stopped talking from the moment you arrived. It's because no one comes and sees me these days. Can you believe it that I sometimes find no one to talk to so I find myself chatting away to my chickens just in case I forget how to talk? Anyway, when I began to grow up my eyes opened to the world more and I understood its ways and how the Lord had ordered His creation. On certain days my father would take us to the field, and he and Awwad would put the seeds in the furrow and Nazeera and I would cover them over with earth afterwards. Through the power of the Lord, with water and sun, the little seeds would with the days break through the earth and become all sorts and kinds of blessings, some beans, some maize, some I-don't-know-what. I also noticed that the cats and the dogs, and the donkeys and the rabbits and the goats would jump onto each other and have children. Bit by bit I was able to understand how the same thing went on between men and women, and that those of their children who died died by Allah's will, and those of their children who lived lived by Allah's will, and that, in His wisdom, for every one that died there was always another one to take his place. I realized that Allah the Sublime had in this manner given the female the task of continuing His creation. Isn't that so? Isn't it we who are pregnant for nine months and give suck to the child and worry about it till it grows strong, while the man's part in the whole affair is just one night of fun? When I'd understood these things I'd stay awake at night and listen to my mother and father – may Allah forgive me. Of course the whole of life wasn't all misery and not having enough to eat and being beaten. There were times when I enjoyed myself, specially when I'd steal off on my own among the fields and sit down and play alongside the water channel and make things out of mud and leave them in the sun to dry. At first I made little pots and pans and water jars, and then I tried to make cats and dogs and birds. One day I said to myself 'Why don't I make my mother and father.' I made both of them with arms and legs and a head and then I put a thing like a cat's tail on my father. I didn't know what to put for my mother, so I lifted my *galabia* and didn't find anything there except for something lying there between two leaves, all hidden away inside, something like a sort of mulberry. Then early one day as I was about to go out to have a look at my mud things and see whether or not they'd dried yet in the sun, I found the women coming in and gathering round, and then they took hold of me and forced my legs open and cut away the mulberry with a razor. They left me with a wound in my body and another wound deep inside me, a feeling that a wrong had been done to me, a wrong that could never be undone. And so the tears welled up in my eyes once again. When the wound in my body healed my mother said to me that the time had come for me to go to the Qur'anic school so as to learn about my religion. I was happy about this and thought I'd just play around a bit, but the Sheikh we had used to beat us on the soles of our feet whenever one of us made a mistake in a single word and would shout at us: 'Girl, pronounce it right – this is the Qur'an not just any old words. If you don't you'll go to Hell.' Then one day I suddenly found the wound was bleeding again, so I ran to my mother and told her: 'See

9

what you've done to me!' She told me this was the period and that I was now all ready to be a bride. She took hold of me and tied a belt round my middle and a piece of old cloth between my legs and said to me that from now on I had to be careful and keep away from boys. So I began putting kohl on my eyes and tying the kerchief over my head at a jaunty angle and making a noise with my anklets as I walked along in my coloured sandals. By this time I'd found my breasts had swollen and become like pomegranates and when I walked they'd bounce about and there was no controlling them. I swear to you the boys went crazy when they used to see me. But it was Hamdan who really loved me. He used to sit under the sycamore tree in front of our house and sing the *mawwal*[2] about Bahiyya's eyes so that the whole village came to know he was singing it to me. Of course I'd known him from when I was young and often we'd played together, but when we grew up we looked at one another with different eyes. He would follow me about wherever I went, keeping at a distance, and we never had the courage to speak to each other. Only the way he looked at me told me of his love for me. And what nights I spent dreaming of him and telling myself that this was the man who'd make me feel glad I was born a woman! These were the happiest days I passed in my whole life, for there's no happier time for a girl than when her heart's still green and full of hopes. Then suddenly all these hopes were shattered when my father came in one day and said to me: 'Congratulations, Bahiyya, we've read the Fatiha[3] for you with Dahshan.' What a black day that was! I just sat where I was and cried. I didn't dare say I wanted to marry Hamdan or even to look up at my father. I was an ignorant girl and who was I to say I wanted this man and not that one? He'd have cut my throat for me. So I told myself that my destiny was with Dahshan and that was that. And what shall I tell you, daughter, about my life with him, and he your father who was taken from me and passed away when you were still a child at my breast? I wasn't all that happy with him, perhaps because of the bilharzia that was eating away at his strength, or perhaps the reason was what those women did to me with the razor when I was a young girl. After he died I found myself in a different position. All my life I'd been ruled by a man, first my father and then my husband. I thought when he died I'd be free and on my own and would do as I liked. The trouble was though that I'd still got some life in me and was still young and I didn't find a hand stretched out to me as I struggled to bring you up, especially as your Uncle Awwad had travelled abroad and your Aunt Nazeera had married and gone off to another village so that I was like a branch that has been lopped off a tree, all alone and like a stranger in my own village. At that time I felt that a woman without a man was like a fish out of water among people, and the women would look at her as a danger to their men and you'd find them keeping away from her as though she were a dog with the mange. But what's the point, daughter, of going on talking? A man's still a man and a woman will remain a woman whatever she does. Anyway, here you are, daughter mine, and Allah willing you'll be staying with me for a few days. Just let's hope the good Lord allows me to end my days before I become completely blind and helpless and a burden to my children. Daughter, I'm not crying now because I'm fed up or regret that the Lord created me a woman. No, it's not that. It's just that I'm sad about my life and my youth that have come and gone without my knowing how to live them really and truly as a woman.

Notes

1. There is a traditional song of this title which tells of the beauty of the eyes of a peasant girl called Bahiyya.
2. A poem in the colloquial language.
3. The Fatiha, or first short chapter of the Qur'an, is read when a marriage contract is made.

Telephone Call

From a nearby flat a telephone rings and rings, then stops, and the number is redialled and the ringing starts again, then stops, then starts again. What desperate contact is someone trying to make at this hour of the night? Is it a matter of life or death, or perhaps one of love? There is nothing like love to induce such a state of despair, no other reason to explain such obstinacy: a lover has been left and seeks the opportunity to plead to be allowed back. He must know that his beloved is at the other end and is refusing to pick up the receiver.

And here I am sitting for hours alone in my flat, knowing there is no one to ring, that there is no question of pleading or submitting to any terms, for there is no way of communicating from the grave. Does not everyone try to find some glimmer of hope even in the darkest situations? Does not the man standing on the scaffold hope that some miracle will, in the few seconds left, save him? Is not history full of such miracles? And yet I don't really ask for a miracle, nothing as tangible as that, just the very smallest of signs that he is there beyond the grave waiting for me. A small sign that I would understand and I would seek nothing further after that. Why, for instance, couldn't the vase of artificial flowers change its place from the small table by the window and I wake from sleep to find it on top of the bookcase? It is so little to ask.

The telephone has stopped ringing. Has the caller accepted his fate? Or has he sought temporary peace in sleep? It's late. The black head of night is being streaked with grey. These next few hours are the only ones during which Cairo knows a short period of quiet, a time when even the solitary cars that are about don't find it necessary to hoot. Outside the window the street is deserted except for the few cats that scavenge in peace at night and snatch their hours of sleep in the daytime.

Soon the call to dawn prayers will float like clouds of sound across the sleeping city. I shall hear it from three different mosques that surround our building. The calls will follow one another not quite synchronized, so that when one is pronouncing the *shahadah*[1], another will be telling me that 'prayer is better than sleep' – I who spend my nights awake.

The night around me is pregnant with a silence that speaks of memories. The familiar objects tell me of the life I lived so fully and which, with his death, has come to a sudden stop. Since then I have been waiting. Otherwise, what is the significance of the forty days after death? Has it not come down to us from the Pharaohs, those experts on death, that during these days the dead are still hovering around us and only later take themselves off elsewhere? If he is to communicate, then it must surely be during this period, for after that we shall truly be in two separate worlds.

I must try to stop myself from thinking of the terrible changes being wrought on that face and body I loved so much. How often had I prayed that I might die first and be spared the struggle to continue in life without him.

As usual I am waiting for the call to dawn prayers, after which I shall go to my bedroom and sleep for a few hours. The maid will let herself into the flat with her own key, clean up, bring in the necessities for life and put them in the fridge, take the money I leave for her, and depart. This is the only way to live at present, to turn life upside down, to sleep, with the aid of sleeping pills, during the hours when life is being led, and to be awake with my thoughts of him when the world around me is sleeping: to turn life upside down and thus to be partly dead to it.

The silence is torn apart by the ringing of the telephone. Ever since he died the telephone has been silent, except perhaps during the day when the maid would answer and tell the caller that her mistress was not available and did not want any calls. But who would ring at such an hour? As the noise bored into my ears I suddenly knew the significance of the call. No, it would not be his voice at the other end; things were done more subtly than that. I knew exactly what would happen.

I walked towards the little side table, the one we'd bought together, and with a steady hand raised the receiver to my ear. As I had expected, no voice broke the silence. I held it closer to my ear, thinking that maybe there would be the sound of breathing, but even this I told myself would not happen. What was happening demanded a high degree of faith on my part. Life and death were both a matter of faith. As I held the receiver tightly against my ear it was as though, like the Sufi image of the water taking on the colour of its container, I were being poured from a container of black despair into one of light-filled hope and confidence. And so I sat holding a soundless receiver to my ear for what might have been minutes or hours. In such circumstances, what is time? Then, suddenly, the spell was broken and the line went dead. I woke from my reverie to the first words of the call to prayer seeping through into the room.

I rose and made my ablutions, then returned to the living room, spread out my prayer carpet and performed the dawn prayer. As I sat with my prayer-beads, I was conscious of being enveloped in a cloak of contentment and gratitude. I knew for certain that all was right.

The all-pervading silence was shattered by the ringing of the telephone again, more blaring and insistent than the first time. I tried to will it to stop, for I felt an instinctive reluctance to answer it. After sitting for so long with my prayer-beads, my legs were stiff and shook with exhaustion as I walked across the room to the telephone. In trepidation I picked up the receiver and the voice of the operator immediately greeted me:

'Good morning, madam. I'm sorry for the call you had some

minutes ago. It was a call from abroad and the call was put through to you by mistake. Please accept our apologies for waking you at this hour.'

'It doesn't matter,' I said and replaced the receiver.

I went back and sat down again on the prayer carpet. My hand was trembling as the prayer-beads ran through my fingers and I kept on asking pardon of the Almighty. Only now was I aware of the enormity of what I had sought from Him and which, in my simplicity, I had thought He had granted: a sign from the beyond. Then I was reminded of how when the Prophet, on whom be the blessings and peace of God, died, the Muslims were plunged into consternation and disbelief by the news and of Abu Bakr's words to them: 'For those of you who worship Muhammed, Muhammed is dead; and for those who worship Allah, Allah is alive and dies not.'

Though the tears were running down my cheeks, I finally felt at peace with myself in submitting to what the Almighty had decreed.

Note

1. The doctrinal formula in Islam.

Thursday Lunch

~~~~~~

As the door of the flat closed behind Kareem and he left for the office, I arranged the pillows behind my back and burst into tears, crying as I had not done since childhood. Then I remembered his final words before leaving: 'Don't forget it's Thursday,' so I rose heavily and sat myself in front of the dressing-table mirror. I was not happy at what I saw: a woman clearly past her best. I had recently celebrated – if that is the right word – my fiftieth birthday. All fifty years, I felt, were shown in the footprints they had left round my eyes, which were still my best feature, and in the slackness round my chin. Only the mouth appeared to have escaped the ravages of time with its full and sensual lips. As for my body, though slim when compared to many women of my age, it had borne the burden of bearing three children and each had ploughed deeper at the furrows made by the one before him. Nowadays I no longer looked at the mirror when I changed my clothes.

I had been lying in bed staring up at the ceiling while my husband had dressed. I had told him I had a headache and that I'd have my breakfast later. I had thought how sad it was that one could approach the end of life and find that for all the people who were around him there was not in fact anyone to whom one could go in a time of crisis and unburden oneself; that instead of building up relationships with an increasing number of friends as time went by, we find ourselves collecting around us a small number of acquaintances, some of whom we positively dislike, and at the same time make barriers between ourselves and those nearest to us. Who was there to whom I could talk frankly about my problem? To my son Adel, who was at an age when he had become wholly self-centred and for whom his mother was no more than the person who demanded from time to time that he tidy up his room? To my daughter Suha who was busy bringing up a young family? To the youngest, Sameh, preoccupied with his studies and the football team? How to tell them that the relationship between their father and I no longer contained that essential ingredient of marriage. Anyway, a mother did not discuss such things with her children.

While I dressed sluggishly, plunging myself into the blackest of moods, the servant girl Attiyat knocked at the door and entered. I had tired of telling her that there was no point in knocking at the door if one didn't wait for an answer before entering.

'We're out of gas,' she said in her abrupt way.

'And the spare cylinder?'

She shook her head apathetically.

'Haven't I told you a hundred times that we must always have a full spare cylinder? Why didn't you tell me before? Go down and get someone to bring one at once.'

She knew very well that today was Thursday, the day I went to my mother's for lunch, and that I'd be leaving shortly and wouldn't be back till the afternoon and had thus assured herself a long break. I looked in my handbag and gave her two pounds.

'Give the change to the man.'

'Yes,' she said, and a moment later I heard the front door slam. I felt alone and deserted, even by the servant, and started to cry again. Then, becoming aware that I must be at my mother's shortly, I made an effort to pull myself together. I made the decision to leave early and to walk to my mother's, for, though it was a long way, the walk would do me good and then at least I wouldn't have to worry about trying to find a taxi to take me to the other side of Zamalek.[1]

I walked for a long time in the side streets but didn't feel tired for I was preoccupied with my own world. It was when I had almost arrived at the building of which my mother occupied the top floor that I was shaken from my reverie by a high-pitched screech that was suddenly stifled. I looked up in alarm to see a man in a soiled *galabia* pass a knife across the neck of a chicken and throw it into a can, which he covered over with a wooden board. As I passed the cart which supported the stacked palm-branch cages of chickens awaiting customers, I heard the frenzied thumping of the chicken against the sides of the can. I felt physically sick and hurried past. I hoped that my mother wouldn't be having chicken for lunch.

The prospect of spending three or more hours with her appalled me. How closed in and self-contained she was! With the years I had felt that the gap between our ages had narrowed and that we had become no more than two old ladies. Was it not therefore strange that a closer and less rigid relationship had not developed between us? Yet, in her presence, I was still that little girl who didn't dare tell her when she had had her first period and instead confided in her elder sister, with whom I had remained so close until her recent death. Who, though, was to blame? I who didn't find the courage or my mother who made me feel that courage was needed to face her? Perhaps the reason for the gulf that separated us was that she was the product of a different upbringing and had lived in times that were easier; her childhood had been utterly different from mine, for she was of Turkish origin and had been brought up by a French governess before marrying my father at an early age and coming to Cairo. And Cairo at that time was an elegant city for those with money.

The spacious drawing room with its many side tables and elaborately framed mirrors that reflected the portraits of tarbushed and turbaned personalities who had played their part in Egypt's history, and the bibelots brought back from Turkey or Europe, and the expensive Persian carpets, was strikingly out of character with the ragged city that lay beyond the walls of the flat. It was even out of character with the building itself in which my mother had lived for so long and which, with its marble entrance and double stairway, had become shabby. My mother in her elegant, air-conditioned flat, was like a patient with severe allergies who lives encapsulated in an atmosphere that is sterilized against the outside world.

She rose from her favourite chair to greet me, supporting herself on the stick she used ever since she had slipped on the parquet. Her thin body was upright and her complexion seemed apparently to be without wrinkles; her silvery hair was carefully arranged. She was dressed as usual in a white silk blouse and dark skirt. She looked at her watch:

'To the dot,' she said with a smile.

'I walked,' I said.

She held me by the shoulder and we touched cheeks.

'You poor thing, you couldn't find a taxi?'

Before I could answer she had launched into one of her diatribes about how the traffic problem in Cairo was getting worse and that it was even pointless to own a car. Her information on this topic, as on many others, was derived solely from the newspapers.

'Does Kareem still drive?'

'Of course,' I said, 'but there's someone at the office whose job it is to find a place to park it in.'

Muhammedain, the Nubian servant, entered; he had been in her service from when he was a young lad helping the house-boy Mustafa, from the time she was first married. He brought two glasses of lemon juice and we asked after each other's health in the same phrases we used every Thursday.

'And how are you all?'

'Thanks be to God, Muhammedain.'

'May God keep them and bless them, madam.'

I sipped at the lemon juice which, to my taste, never had enough sugar in it.

'And how's Adel?' asked my mother. 'Working hard? He takes his finals this year, doesn't he?'

'No, Mummy, next year.'

'That's excellent. And Suha and her husband and the children? And Sameh?'

'They're all fine.'

'Thanks be to God,' she said, and at that moment Muhammedain appeared in the glass doorway to announce that lunch was ready, and I walked slowly beside her between the islands of carpets supporting occasional tables amidst the sea of glowing parquet.

The meal started with cold consommé, then Muhammedain brought in a large fish that he had done in the oven with onions, raisins and pine nuts. My mother enquired of me in French – Muhammedain was standing behind her chair – how much one paid for eggs these days and began comparing the prices of them long ago with today's. I found myself being reminded of the slaughtered chicken in the can and I said to my mother: 'I don't think I can eat a thing more after that delicious fish,' and I smiled up at Muhammedain as he removed my plate. Once Muhammedain had left the room my mother informed me that he had prepared us some skewers of kebab and that he'd been blowing away since morning at the charcoal out on the balcony and that he'd be offended if we didn't eat some, so I ate some pieces of lamb kebab and we then ended up with crême caramel. I decided that for supper I'd just have fruit after that heavy meal. How, I asked myself in astonishment, did my mother manage to eat all this? Did she eat like this every day or was it just on Thursdays that she celebrated my presence with her?

We returned to the drawing room to have our coffee and my mother talked about how unfair it was for young people today and of the difficulty they had in finding homes and that girls often had to waste their best years waiting till they could get married. Her voice, though, betrayed no real emotion and it was as if she were talking about some film she'd seen on television. I thought how distant and separated we were, each one of us in her own world. I wished that it were possible, just for once, for us to make contact and for me to talk openly to her about my bewilderment as I faced a problem whose dimensions I couldn't define. I knew, though, that this was out of the question, and the wish was suddenly replaced by a pressing desire to escape. I reminded myself that etiquette demanded that I wait till my mother indicated that I should leave. I was taken out of my thoughts by my mother's voice saying:

'Do you know what today is?'

'Thursday?' I answered in surprise.

'No, I mean the date.'

'Today's the . . .'

'Today's the twentieth of May, the anniversary of your father's death.' She spoke quietly, her eyes lowered. 'Today is twenty-four years since he died, and not a day has passed without my thinking of him.'

As I met my mother's gaze I saw that her eyes were unnaturally bright and realized with astonishment that they had filled with tears. I was at a loss as to what to do, but I was saved any decision by my mother rising to her feet.

'Now's the time for me to have my rest. God willing, we'll meet up next Thursday, if I'm given life till then.'

She gave a short dry laugh and brushed her cheek against mine. I shut the door of the flat behind me and pressed on the button for the lift. The thought came to me that Kareem was most likely already home and that hopefully I'd find a taxi to take me back.

Note

1. High-class residential district of Cairo.

An Incident in the Ghobashi Household

~~~~~~

Zeinat woke to the strident call of the red cockerel from the rooftop above where she was sleeping. The Ghobashi house stood on the outskirts of the village and in front of it the fields stretched out to the river and the railway track.

The call of the red cockerel released answering calls from neighbouring rooftops. Then they were silenced by the voice of the *muezzin* from the lofty minaret among the mulberry trees calling: 'Prayer is better than sleep.'

She stretched out her arm to the pile of children sleeping alongside her and tucked the end of the old rag-woven *kilim* round their bodies, then shook her eldest daughter's shoulder.

'It's morning, another of the Lord's mornings. Get up, Ni'ma – today's market day.'

Ni'ma rolled onto her back and lazily stretched herself. Like someone alerted by the sudden slap of a gust of wind, Zeinat stared down at the body spread out before her. Ni'ma sat up and pulled her *galabia* over her thighs, rubbing at her sleep-heavy eyes in the rounded face with the prominent cheekbones.

'Are you going to be able to carry the grain to the market, daughter, or will it be too heavy for you?'

'Of course, mother. After all, who else is there to go?'

Zeinat rose to her feet and went out with sluggish steps to the courtyard, where she made her ablutions. Having finished the ritual prayer, she remained in the seated position as she counted

23

off on her fingers her glorifications of Allah. Sensing that Ni'ma was standing behind her, she turned round to her:

'What are you standing there for? Why don't you go off and get the tea ready?'

Zeinat walked towards the corner where Ghobashi had stored the maize crop in sacks; he had left them as a provision for them after he had taken his air ticket from the office that had found him work in Libya and which would be bringing him back in a year's time.

'May the Lord keep you safe while you're away, Ghobashi,' she muttered.

Squatting in front of a sack, the grain measure between her thighs, she scooped up the grain with both hands till the measure was full, then poured it into a basket. Coughing, she waved away the dust that rose up to her face, then returned to her work.

The girl went to the large clay jar, removed the wooden covering and dipped the mug into it and sprinkled water on her face; she wetted the tips of her fingers and parted her plaits, then tied her handkerchief over her head. She turned to her mother:

'Isn't that enough, mother? What do we want the money for?'

Zeinat struck her knees with the palms of her hands and tossed her head back.

'Don't we have to pay off Hamdan's wage? — or was he cultivating the beans for us for nothing, just for the fun of hard work?'

Ni'ma turned away and brought the stove from the window shelf, arranging the dried corn-cobs in a pyramid and lighting them. She put it alongside her mother, then filled the teapot with water from the jar and thrust it into the embers. She squatted down and the two sat in silence. Suddenly Zeinat said:

'Since when has the buffalo been with young?'

'From after my father went away.'

'That's to say, right after the Great Feast, daughter?'

Ni'ma nodded her head in assent, then lowered it and began drawing lines in the dust.

24

'Why don't you go off and see how many eggs have been laid while the tea's getting ready.'

Zeinat gazed into the glow of the embers. She had a sense of peace as she stared into the dancing flames. Ghobashi had gone and left the whole load on her shoulders: the children, the two *kirats* of land and the buffalo. 'Take care of Ni'ma,' he had said the night before he left. 'The girl's body has ripened.' He had then spread out his palms and said: 'O Lord, for the sake of the Prophet's honour, let me bring back with me a marriage dress for her of pure silk.' She had said to him: 'May your words go straight from your lips to Heaven's gate, Ghobashi.' He wouldn't be returning before the following Great Feast. What would happen when he returned and found out the state of affairs? She put her head between the palms of her hands and leaned over the fire, blowing away the ashes. 'How strange,' she thought, 'are the girls of today! The cunning little thing was hanging out her towels at the time of her period every month just as though nothing had happened, and here she is in her fourth month and there's nothing showing.'

Ni'ma returned and untied the cloth from round the eggs, put two of them in the fire and the rest in a dish. She then brought two glasses and the tin of sugar and sat down next to her mother, who was still immersed in her thoughts.

'Didn't you try to find some way out?'

Ni'ma hunched her shoulders in a gesture of helplessness.

'Your father's been gone four months. Isn't there still time?'

'What's the use? If only the Lord were to spare you the trouble of me. Wouldn't it be for the best, mother, if my foot were to slip as I was filling the water jar from the canal and we'd be done with it?'

Zeinat struck herself on the breast and drew her daughter to her.

'Don't say such a wicked thing. Don't listen to such promptings of the Devil. Calm down and let's find some solution before your father returns.'

Zeinat poured out the tea. In silence she took quick sips at it, then put the glass in front of her and shelled the egg and bit into it.

25

Ni'ma sat watching her, her fingers held round the hot glass. From outside came the raised voices of women discussing the prospects at the day's market, while men exchanged greetings as they made their way to the fields. Amidst the voices could be heard Hamdan's laughter as he led the buffalo to the two *kirats* of land surrounding the house.

'His account is with Allah,' muttered Zeinat. 'He's fine and doesn't have a worry in the world.'

Ni'ma got up and began winding round the end of her headcloth so as to form a pad on her head. Zeinat turned round and saw her preparing herself to go off to the market. She pulled her by her *galabia* and the young girl sat down again. At this moment they heard knocking at the door and the voice of their neighbour, Umm al-Khair, calling:

'Good health to you, folk. Isn't Ni'ma coming with me to market as usual, Auntie Zeinat? Or isn't she up yet?'

'Sister, she's just going off to stay with our relatives.'

'May Allah bring her back safely.'

Ni'ma looked at her mother enquiringly, while Zeinat placed her finger to her mouth. When the sound of Umm al-Khair's footsteps died away, Ni'ma whispered:

'What are you intending to do, mother? What relatives are you talking about?'

Zeinat got up and rummaged in her clothes box and took out a handkerchief tied round some money, also old clothes. She placed the handkerchief in Ni'ma's palm and closed her fingers over it.

'Take it – they're my life savings.'

Ni'ma remained silent as her mother went on:

'Get together your clothes and go straight away to the station and take a ticket to Cairo. Cairo's a big place, daughter, where you'll find protection and a way to make a living till Allah brings you safely to your time. Then bring it back with you at dead of night without anyone seeing you or hearing you.'

Zeinat raised the end of her *galabia* and put it between her teeth. Taking hold of the old clothes, she began winding them round her waist. Then she let fall the *galabia*. Ni'ma regarded her in astonishment:

'And what will we say to my father?'

'It's no time for talking. Before you go off to the station, help me up with the basket so that I can go to the market for people to see me like this. Isn't it better, when he returns, for your father to find himself with a legitimate son than an illegitimate grandson?'

Badriyya and Her Husband

~~~~~~

In the orange glow of sunset Badriyya made out the sturdy figure of her husband amidst the group of men making their leisurely way down the lane from the main street where the buses thundered past. He was talking and gesticulating, while those around him were laughing and turning to each other. She thought he looked thinner than before and that he walked heavily for a young man of his age. She was pleased when Hanafi the butcher, a man well known for his haughtiness, stopped stripping cuts of meat from the carcases that hung in front of his shop and, wiping his hands on his apron, went up to the young man and shook him warmly by the hand. The men continued on till they passed by the shop of Umm Gabir, who had poked out her head between the boxes stacked up on the counter in front of her.

Badriyya was standing at the window of her mother's bedroom while her mother was kneeling on her bed and gripping the window ledge, as they both looked from the top of the building where they lived in a small flat that had been built to one side of the roof. As Omar passed, Badriyya hoped that he would turn and notice her at the window. But the group passed by and went on down the lane until they turned off and disappeared into the intersecting lane. Badriyya realized that they were making their way to the café to celebrate her husband's return; the café of Master Zaki with whom Omar used to work. It was at this same café, late one evening, that the police had entered and arrested him.

Tears of joy welled into her eyes as she sat alongside her mother on the bed. She pictured Omar now at the café, no longer serving others, but the centre of attention, with Master Zaki opening bottles of Pepsi-Cola and Seven-Up in his honour. Suddenly she became aware of the presence of her mother. She turned and looked at the withered face and the nose that almost touched the jutting chin, and the small bright eyes.

'Honestly, anyone seeing him would think Antar[1] himself had come back to life. All that's missing is for them to have brought him in on a white horse.'

As the old woman spoke these words she saw the look of distress that flickered across her daughter's face. Receiving no reply, she continued: 'Anyone would think he was returning from freeing Palestine. It wouldn't be so bad if he'd been doing a worthwhile job – not stealing a couple of old tyres that wouldn't fetch fifty piastres.'

The old woman gave a cackling laugh. 'As the proverb says, "If you steal, steal a camel." The boy's not just a criminal but a fool as well. When they took him away you cried and now when he's come back you're crying again.'

'Because I'm so happy, Ma. My man's come back to me at last.'

The old woman gripped the edge of the bed with her claw-like hand and Badriyya put her own gently on it. The old woman gave her daughter a blank stare.

'Please, Ma, please try to understand. Omar's not really bad and now more than ever he needs help and understanding from us both. He always used to feel that you were against our marrying. It would help him a lot if he felt that you wished us well.'

'After I saw you were determined to marry him, what could I do but accept the fact? What do you think I want for my daughter except that the good Lord give her happiness in marriage? You're free to live as you like with whom you like, and soon the Lord will be sparing you the trouble of me.'

'Why, Ma, bring up such things now? This is a night for

being in a good mood.'

Her mother made a loud sucking noise with her lips and withdrew her hand from her daughter's.

'I was frightened for you during these past years. What would people say of a young girl living on her own with her man in prison? You know that no one's safe from what people say. If there's no story to tell they make one up just for the fun of it. Now your man's back and there's no need for me any longer.'

She half closed an eye and gave her daughter a quick sideways glance.

'Are you going to be finding the time for looking after me?'

'Don't say such a thing, Ma. God willing, all three of us will live together happily.'

The old woman shook her head in rejection.

'Isn't it a pity I didn't get pregnant during the few days we lived together before they took him away? He'd be coming back to a child of his own.'

When the mother made no comment, Badriyya added: 'Really, Ma, wouldn't you like to see your daughter with a son?'

'It'd be sure to take after him.'

Badriyya got up and went to the bathroom, a corner of which was used as a kitchen. She returned with a glass of warm milk. The mother began sipping at the milk, her head lowered to the glass. The call to evening prayer was given from the nearby Mosque of al-Shafie. Badriyya waited till her mother had finished the milk, then she put her to bed and covered her up, and closed the window. She went to her own room where she put on the new nightdress she had bought for the night of his return and sat herself in the small hallway by the door. After a while she heard his footsteps as he felt his way up to the roof. She put on the light and opened the door of the flat. She realized immediately that he was drunk, swaying and out of breath. She helped him through the doorway and clasped him to her.

'How are you, Badriyya?' he asked thickly.

'I'm well, love. Thank God for your safe return.'

'I'm fine. I'm great. The lads gave me a great welcome. How's your mother?'

'She's gone to bed. She stayed up for you, but then she went to sleep.'

'Just as well – I'm not up to taking her snide remarks.'

He went into their room and stretched himself out on the bed. He put his hands behind his head and watched her smilingly as she took off his shoes.

'I'm dead tired,' he said, and fumbled in his jacket and produced a packet of cigarettes and matches. He offered her one but she shook her head.

'I don't smoke – have you forgotten or what?'

'Yes, I forgot. In prison one's only worry is how to get hold of a cigarette.' He moved his body and patted the bed alongside him. 'Sit down,' he said.

'D'you know,' he said, 'you haven't changed at all?'

'Honestly?'

'Honestly.'

He put out his hand to her and she held it for a while as she gazed down at his handsome features.

'It was a long and tiring day.'

Hardly were the words out of his mouth than his head lolled onto his shoulder and he was asleep. She lay down alongside him and pulled the coverlet over herself. She was grateful that her mother had not witnessed the state he was in. She lay on her back and stared up into the darkness. She felt fully awake and that, despite having to be up early to go to her work in the workshop in Khan al-Khalili, she would sleep little that night.

Their love affair had been as sudden and romantic as the films she went to and which provided her with an escape from her bitter reality. She had on several occasions noticed the young man who served at the café and it was not, therefore, as though a complete stranger had followed her into the cinema and sat down beside her. It was a film she had seen several times before and she was pleased when he remarked to her that it was the best Egyptian film he'd ever seen. When he'd suggested that they meet up next Friday and go together to the latest film featuring the same actor, she had agreed. Right from the beginning she had felt, like the heroine in the film, that here was the man of her dreams, the man who would rescue her from a life that stretched ahead like a long dark tunnel. Omar told her that he was working temporarily at Master Zaki's café so as to gain experience and that he would then take his share of the land he had inherited from his father in Beni Sueif and that he planned to open a café of his own in some high-class district, a place where people came with their wives, not a place like Master Zaki's where most of the tables and chairs stood in the lane itself and the clients were workmen and impoverished junior government employees sitting all evening over a single order and playing backgammon or dominoes. She enjoyed listening to his plans for the future, for she liked a young man to be ambitious. A few Fridays after their first meeting he had proposed marriage to her and they had agreed that he would come next week, after Friday prayers, to visit her mother and that she would arrange for her uncle who lived in Boulak to be there. While the meeting between Omar and her uncle had not been a success – after Omar had left, the uncle had expressed the view that he was 'all talk and hot air' – Badriyya made it clear that her mind was made up. Her uncle had therefore wished her all happiness and had placed a five pound note in her hand as a wedding present. And so she had married Omar and he had moved with his suitcase of clothes into the room that served Badriyya as a bedroom and in which she and her mother ate on a small table set in one corner.

The single month they had spent together before he was taken away merely opened her appetite for something that remained unknown and untried deep within her. She was like a piece of land that has been prepared for sowing and suddenly left.

A few weeks after Omar had been imprisoned Badriyya had returned from work to find her uncle sitting with her mother awaiting her. Without any preliminaries or wasting of time they had told her that Omar was a wastrel, a good-for-nothing, who had merely been looking for a roof over his head and a woman to look after him. Her uncle informed her that she had the right to divorce Omar and that he knew a decent man who had recently been widowed who would be pleased to marry her directly she was divorced. But Badriyya had been adamant: she would wait for Omar. After all, who was there to stand by a man in bad times but his wife?

'Love is really blind,' her mother had said and had turned to her brother with a shrug of her shoulders, so Badriyya's uncle had got up, kissed her on the forehead, given her two pounds and left with the words: 'As you like. If you change your mind, tell your mother.'

The morning after Omar's return from prison Badriyya rose as usual at dawn, prepared breakfast for herself and her mother and went off to work. Omar did not stir in the bed.

On returning from work at five o'clock Badriyya found Omar sitting alongside her mother on the bed, while the two laughed, played cards and smoked. She was surprised, for she had never seen her mother in such a good mood.

'He made me some really excellent coffee,' said the old woman, laughing. 'It's as though he put something into it.'

'Honestly, I didn't, Ma,' he said, laughing and looking at Badriyya. 'The stuff's really expensive these days. The bit of hashish or opium we were able to get hold of in prison wasn't enough to make one high after we'd divided it up among us.'

He took Badriyya by the hand and got to his feet.

'Sit down and rest, Badriyya, and I'll go and make us all some coffee. Maybe I'm not much good at some things but I didn't work in a coffee shop for nothing.'

'Can you imagine, Badriyya,' said her mother, when Omar had left, 'he's turned out to be a real nice fellow. Directly he heard me coughing he came along with a glass of water and went on tapping me on the back till I'd got my breath back.' She cackled with laughter. 'And then he brought a pack of cards and showed me all the tricks he'd learnt in prison.'

As they sat drinking the coffee Omar told them of some of the types he'd met in prison.

'You'd be wrong if you thought that everyone in jail is either a criminal or a fool. Many's the man that gets put into prison through no fault of his own. For instance, take Helmi Effendi. When I arrived he'd already been there a couple of years and got out before me a month or two ago. He's a contractor and sells sanitary ware. He buys and sells for hundreds of thousands. They accused him of trading in stolen goods. What fault is it of his if the merchants bring him things from here and there? But Helmi Effendi's no fool – even the warders had more respect for him than for the Governor himself. Don't think that when he came out he was sitting at the mosque door. No, he's got his money tucked away and his business was going on even when he was in prison. He's got a villa and a car and he's sending it tonight to take me to his place. "Omar," he said to me, "the day you come out, put your trust in the Almighty and in me. I'll not forget the friends I had when times were bad." '

'But I thought, Omar, we'd spend the evening together,' protested Badriyya, 'and I've prepared some pigeons stuffed with rice.'

'And you can make a real night of it,' said the mother, laughing and winking at Omar. He joined in the laughter and pointed a finger at the old woman:

'I now know where Badriyya's got her naughtiness from' – and the three of them laughed together.

Omar found that he'd run out of cigarettes, so he asked Badriyya to go down to get him a packet of Marlboro. She protested she didn't have any money and he said that he too was skint. She suggested that he might at least smoke some local brand at half the price.

'And what sort of impression would that make on Helmi Effendi?' he answered her, turning to the mother.

'That's right,' said the old woman. 'Everything's got its price, Badriyya. One day soon Helmi Effendi'll find him a splendid job.

Go and get him a packet of Marlboro from Umm Gaber's on tick till the good Lord fixes things up.'

When Badriyya returned with the packet of cigarettes he gave one to her mother and lit it for her, then stuffed a couple of cigarettes under her pillow. Then he went to the bathroom and washed and shaved again and put on a clean shirt. The two women leaned out of the window and followed him with their eyes as he made his way up the lane towards the main street where a car waited for him.

From then on Omar came back late night after night. He would return in a state of exhaustion from drink or drugs and would flop down on the bed and sleep fully clothed till late the next morning. On one occasion he stayed out all night, returning towards dawn, and Badriyya began being worried lest the police return and put him in handcuffs again. She waited in vain for him to approach her, and whenever she alluded to the question he would find some excuse and would tell her there was plenty of time for such things, and that the important thing was for him to give his time to the project that was occupying his thoughts and that would provide them with a decent life and would save her from going out to work, and that his evenings were spent viewing possible sites for the café. As for the time he stayed at home, most of it was spent with the old woman, smoking and chattering and playing cards. One day she archly asked him:

'And when are you two going to give me what I'd like to see before I die?'

'I don't know, Ma. Ask that daughter of yours. She's always tired and fed up.'

That evening, when the mother was alone with Badriyya after Omar had gone out, she asked her about this matter. The rush of blood to Badriyya's face and her silence confirmed, for the mother, Omar's words.

'Watch out, Badriyya,' the old woman told her. 'He's a good-looking boy and every girl would like to have him.'

'I know, Ma,' said Badriyya and immediately got up and went to her room. She asked herself: Had the years of waiting and worrying and working taken their toll of her youth? Was she perhaps no longer attractive? Perhaps, as her mother had hinted, there was another woman. Yet it wasn't reasonable to suppose he'd found someone in these few days.

She made up her mind to speak to him frankly on his return that night.

She felt a desire to go out. She went back to her mother and told her she was going to Umm Gaber's to buy a packet of cigarettes. She descended the long stairway and went out into the lane which lay in darkness except for the glimmer of light that came from the lamp at the corner of the main street. She walked with zigzag steps between the puddles of water and the mounds of garbage. She was seized by a feeling of nausea at the smells of cooking that were diffused from closely packed houses, mingled with the fermentation of urine. She reached Umm Gaber's just as she was about to close the shop. Umm Gaber stretched out a hand with the packet of cigarettes.

'And when's Mr Omar going to buy his cigarettes out of his own pocket?' she muttered.

'God willing, he'll start work soon,' said Badriyya.

Umm Gaber slowly shook her head.

'Wake up, my girl,' she said. 'That husband of yours is no good. Everyone knows what he's really like except you. As the saying goes: "The wife's the last to know." '

Badriyya's hand remained where it was, clasping the packet of cigarettes.

'What do you mean, Umm Gaber? There's some other woman?'

Suddenly Badriyya found Umm Gaber shaking her by the arm:

'Girl, wake up I tell you. The whole place knew about him even before you married. Prison's just made it worse. That husband of yours, if he were a woman, would have been pregnant years ago.'

Badriyya stood staring into Umm Gaber's face for a while as the significance of the words dawned upon her. She left the packet of cigarettes on the counter and turned away. As she walked back she asked herself how it would be possible for her to find the strength not to open the door to him.

Note

1. A legendary poet and hero from pre-Islamic times.

Me and My Sister

~~~~~~

I was puffing as I went into the house because I'd gone up the stairs two at a time so I could get there before my sister though she's older than me. I heard my eldest sister Dalal tell Mummy as they were waiting for us sitting down for lunch that she wanted to go out in the afternoon so as to be at her friend Su'ad's birthday party. Mummy said what she always says: 'What will people say about us when we're on our own without a man in the house?' Dalal replied in a cross way to frighten Mummy because the doctor said that she was upset about Daddy marrying another wife and that we mustn't contradict her. Dalal said the sentence she always says: 'I don't care about people. Let them go hang. They'll talk in any case so how long shall we go on being frightened of them?' When she saw that Mummy was silent and frowning she said she would take me with her so that Mummy needn't worry. Mummy lifted up her hands to the sky and said the prayer she always says: 'May our Lord fix you up with someone decent who'll marry you, Dalal.' I was standing there happy because I like parties but Mummy told me to go off and put away my satchel and wash my hands and come and have lunch with my sisters. So I went off into the bedroom and threw down the satchel and ran off and sat down at table. I was just drinking my soup when Dalal said to me that I'd eaten enough because I had to get on and study before we went out and that she herself would hear my lessons. Mummy was happy about this and got up to go to sleep in her room.

I sat doing my homework and Nagwa went to sleep in the bed we share and Dalal slept beside Sahar in their bed. After a while she got up and stood in front of me and took hold of the history book and asked me to tell her what were the important things Hatshepsut had done. I told her that Queen Hatshepsut had sent the first expedition to the land of Punt through the Red Sea to bring back ebony. Before I had finished what I had to say I felt the pencil hit against my cheek and saw her looking at me with those black eyes of hers which I feel are swallowing me up in a deep dark well. I was shaking with fear and felt terribly humiliated because she'd hit me in the face. From the moment that Sahar had got engaged before her she used to hit me and Nagwa and the servants for the slightest thing. This time I was really upset because I wasn't in the wrong and I couldn't help the tears coming to my eyes. This made her more angry still and she shouted at me: 'Do your lessons properly, you stupid thing.' I lost my temper and snatched the book from her and pointed at the page and said: 'That's what's written.' She didn't read what was said but looked at the picture of Hatshepsut at the top of the page and said: 'You gone blind? There right in front of you it shows Hatshepsut as a man.' I was really annoyed and said to her: 'This Hatshepsut is a lady except she's got a beard.' She looked at the book again then closed it and said: 'Don't be so childish.' Then she told me to wash my face and put on a dress for going out.

Dalal had been at a French school before sitting at home waiting for someone to come and marry her. She used to know about French history only and didn't know anything about the history of Egypt and was even weak in Arabic. I'm clever at it and like it very much and always the teacher leaves my copy book to the end of the lesson and reads out to the girls the composition I've written. Why does Dalal call me stupid when I say things right? I have often heard her say to Mummy that she was wrong to have me after Daddy married again. Mummy spends most of her time in bed and gets up to say her prayers and eat with us then she sits in the bed again and even guests go and see her in her bedroom. Sahar is the one who runs the house and Dalal looks after the expenses so that Mummy and Daddy won't quarrel about them and she's always tough with us about anything we want. When Daddy comes for one night every week he gives us money to buy sweets with and we kiss his hand. He always says to me: 'Do what you're told and it's not right to argue with your older sister.' I keep quiet but I know that she has of course told him everything that has happened during the time he was away but in her own way so that he'll believe her and not give me my pocket money.

I washed my face and quickly put on my best dress then I kissed Dalal on the cheek and said I was sorry and she went out with me holding her by the hand as she swung me along with her walking on her high heels. At the corner behind the house a car drew up beside us and a nice-looking young man opened the door. Dalal pushed me into the back seat and she sat beside him. He raced off till he came to a stop under the shade of a tree far from the street lamp. Dalal then lifted her head which she had kept bent down under the window so no one would see her. The young man asked about me and she said I was her young sister and that she had to bring me because we were a strict family and she couldn't go out alone at night and that though I was young I was very bright and could understand anything that was said and that I might repeat it. Of course I was annoyed at what she said about me though I really am clever but I don't split on anyone. After that Dalal and the young man talked in French and I understood that his name was Mahmoud but I couldn't understand the rest of what they were saying.

Then Mahmoud got out of the car and Dalal turned to me and looked at me with those terrible eyes and said in a voice like the school bell that she would tear my eyes out if I said anything to anyone about meeting a man. She put her red nails right close to my eyes and made me swear by Almighty Allah three times that I would bury the secret deep in a well. I was very frightened and very fed up at the same time because I like to tell everything to my sister Nagwa who is my only friend at home and at school. But

Mahmoud came back and gave Dalal a bottle of perfume and he gave me a big box of chocolates so I forgot about being annoyed. Then we drove in the dark and came out to the desert and the car bumped about on the sands until we saw the light from a wooden kiosk. He came to a stop far from the light and called the shopkeeper and asked for some lemonade. The old man laughed and said: 'The very best quality for the sake of the lady.'

Dalal got down and told me to sit in front and she got in the back and Mahmoud got in beside her. The shopkeeper brought them some cigarettes and they closed all the windows and Dalal told me I could eat as many chocolates as I liked. I put the box on my lap and began eating the chocolates and I only noticed later on the car had filled with the smoke of the cigarettes and it was a funny smell and not at all like the smell of the cigarettes that Mummy and Daddy and their guests used to smoke. I felt giddy and wanted to go to sleep. I heard some dogs barking far away and sounds from the back seat and whispering behind me and I tried to guess what they were doing exactly but I couldn't make it out at all. I got fed up and said to Dalal that I wanted to go back home and that I was sleepy. Mahmoud shouted at me to shut up. I was very frightened and went on calling out to Dalal till she answered me and said we were going to leave. After being annoyed with Mahmoud I was happy about him because suddenly Dalal was talking to me in a friendly way also because he had brought me those lovely chocolates. At last we changed places to go back. All the time I was surprised that the shopkeeper didn't bring us the lemonade we had asked for but had instead brought us cigarettes that no one had asked for but I was too shy to ask.

When we went into the house Mummy called me to her room and asked me where we had been so I told her word for word what Dalal had told me to say: 'We were at Su'ad's house near the club and we ate cakes and drank tea and there weren't any men at all.' I also told the story to Nagwa as I got under the warm blankets but I was furious not to have been able to tell her the truth and she might have been able to tell me why Dalal wanted to sit with Mahmoud in the back seat. I went to sleep and woke up next morning feeling tired but I had to get up and go to school.

After that we met Mahmoud many times and each time I would eat a whole box of chocolates. One night towards the end of winter I heard Dalal saying to Mahmoud that someone had gone to Daddy asking to marry her but that she loved him and that he must go to Daddy before he gave his word to the other man. Mahmoud said to her that he was not thinking of marrying and that he wished her all the best. She got out of the car at once and dragged me with her so hard my arm was going to break.

When the time for the next meeting came she told me to go to him on my own and to keep him busy for an hour until she caught up with us. At the appointed time I went out and walked to the corner. I found him waiting so I got in beside him and bent my head down under the window. He laughed and drove the car as he played with my hair. My hair is longer than Dalal's and it's done up with lovely red ribbons. He asked me about Dalal and I told him she had to go somewhere and that she would be coming after an hour. He asked me where we should go till the time for her to come and I said: 'To the man who sells lemonade of the very best quality for the sake of the lady.' He laughed and said I was nice. I was very happy about this and even more happy because he passed by a sweet shop and bought me a box of chocolates with a picture of a white kitten.

When we got to the kiosk he sat smoking the cigarettes with the car windows closed while I ate the chocolates. I noticed he was fed up so I thought it would be nice to give him a chocolate. When I put one in his mouth he bit my finger and laughed. I laughed too and told him he was naughty. He said: 'Come close so I can see how big you've grown.' So I stood up straight for him to see how tall I was but he pulled me down before I hit my head and sat me on his knees. When he began putting his hand on my chest I rounded my shoulders and felt very ashamed and all my body went hot. He laughed and blew the smoke into my face and I became dizzy and leaned my head against his chest. I felt very happy because for a

43

long time I wanted to sit on Daddy's lap but I was always too frightened to ask him. Daddy of course gave us pocket money but never enough to buy a big box of chocolates like the one Mahmoud gave me. I felt I loved him very much and I kissed him on the cheek but it was as rough as a cactus fruit when we pick them from the bushes in the garden and eat them green. He looked at his watch and said that Dalal would be coming soon so we drove off in the car.

We found her at the corner so I went behind and she got in beside him and we drove through different streets and did not go the same way we always did. Dalal asked him where he was going. He said that he was going to his house which was better than wandering round the streets. She got annoyed and told him to stop the car because she wanted to go back home. He got angry and turned to her and said: 'Perhaps you'd like to tell me where you've been so as to stand me up for an hour?' She said: 'What's it got to do with you? What do you care?' He let go of the steering-wheel and took hold of her hand and said that he loved her and all at once we found ourselves in the hedge of a house. The accident happened in a flash. I hit my head on Dalal's seat and I gave a scream. When I felt my head I found I had a bump as big as a lemon. I saw Dalal and Mahmoud with blood all over their faces and Dalal looking as though she'd fainted away. I went on screaming and calling for Mummy and Mahmoud shouted at me to shut up or I'd bring all the people round us.

Quickly Mahmoud reversed the car and drove it along the road to our house. He stopped at the corner and put the bottle of perfume that was in Dalal's handbag up to her nose. She opened her eyes and told him she couldn't walk all that way so he drove the car right up to our house. We found Mummy and my sisters standing by the windows and staring out into the dark and they saw Mahmoud helping Dalal to the door and quickly returning to his car. Directly we got inside Mummy cleaned up Dalal's wounds and put her into her nightdress and got her into bed. Nagwa helped me into our bed.

When they asked Dalal where we'd been and what had happened and who was the man who had brought us back Dalal pretended she was too dizzy. Then they turned to me but I didn't know what to say so I pretended to be asleep. When we were alone Dalal opened her eyes and for the first time I didn't feel frightened at all. When she smiled at me I thought of the way she used to hit me in the face. I smiled back at her because I knew she wouldn't hit me again. Then I went to sleep.

Mansoura

~~~~~~

Sheikh Zeidan propped his scrawny backside against the pile of sand taken from the trench dug along the length of the street branching off from the central square of one of Cairo's suburbs. Pulling up the ends of his trousers, on top of which he wore a short calico shirt, from his thin legs that were like the branches of a tree from which the bark has been stripped, he engrossed himself in wrapping round them torn pieces of sacking; these he covered over with two nylon bags, binding them all together with bits of string so as to protect himself from the putrid flow from the sewers. The vast iron pipes that he and his fellow workers were to fix in the trench were stacked on both sides of the street.

Jumping into the trench, he gave the signal to the others to start work. They jumped in behind him and spread out through the trench as they awaited the giant yellow bulldozer that was advancing towards them, a pipe suspended on high in its iron grasp that hung down from thick, metal ropes. Slowly it began its descent till it was received by several arms, which guided it to the required place. At this Sheikh Zeidan's voice was raised in a chant:

'O Mansoura, O Allah . . . O Mansoura, O Allah . . . O Mansoura, O Allah.'

Animated, envigorated, the men raised their voices as they intoned the chant in a monotonous rhythm. Even the bulldozer's movements, as it went back and forth, became more energetic, as though it were the leading camel in a caravan moved by the

47

chanting of the camel-driver. It went on bringing one pipe after another to the men in the trench and they would carefully fit the ends together so that the new sewer might come into being. Thus they continued till the sun was extinguished and the sky rusted and work came to a stop; then red warning lamps were hung on the wooden signboards that bore the name of the company entrusted with this work.

When the sky's slate split open to reveal shining stars and the *muezzin* gave the call to evening prayers, the men came out from the tent they'd set up amidst the flowerbeds and lined up behind Sheikh Zeidan. After performing their prayers, they spread out on the damp grass, giving pride of place to their Sheikh. One of the workmen rose and gathered up some broken pieces of scaffolding, making a heap of them in the middle of where they were sitting and set them ablaze and buried the teapot amidst the glowing embers. Soon it was boiling and sending out its fragrance, while the *narghile* was carefully prepared and passed silently from mouth to mouth, each man rubbing his fingers over the mouthpiece before giving it to his neighbour; the puffs were followed by long, noisy gulps from the tin cups filled with dark, generously sugared tea. They sat in a silent circle like men performing some heathen rite. A soft clearing of the throats announced a readiness for the evening's conversation, and they waited for the customary question that was asked whenever a new workman joined them.

Dahshan, who had joined them only that morning, looked round with wondering eyes at the others, then asked abruptly:

'Who's this Mansoura, Sheikh Zeidan, whose name we invoke?'

Sheikh Zeidan gave a smile, and the men exchanged knowing glances as they waited for the Sheikh to begin telling his story as always happened on such occasions. The Sheikh, however, said:

'How extraordinary, fellows! Is there anyone who doesn't know of her great powers?'

Dahshan burst out into a shrill laugh as though excusing himself for his ignorance and said:

'Your pardon, kind people – the fact of the matter is that I'm from a village a long way from where you're from and we don't know about her.'

The men laughed and the Sheikh's eyes gazed distractedly at the blazing fire.

'Good Lord – Mansoura! Is there anyone who hasn't heard of you? Let's say the Fatiha on her soul and a prayer for the Prophet.'

Hands and voices were raised in supplication for mercy for that person who, whenever they fitted a pipe and asked help in her name, seemed to lighten the load for them, as though hidden wings were bearing the pipe along in their stead.

Suddenly the lights of the square came on, dispersing the darkness around them. Sheikh Zeidan clapped his hands together, saying:

'O Light of the Prophet! You see – at the mention of her the light burst forth. There wasn't a prettier girl than her. The way she had of walking brought about an earthquake in men's bodies. Their hearts would tremble as her body, lush as green lettuce, swayed to right and left carrying the earthenware jar of water. She would do the round of the houses, filling up the storage jars of the ladies who were the wives of the leading men of the village. Yes, her clothes might have been shabby but her eyes were glowing lamps. She was a bold one, never lowering her eyes like other girls when facing men. She would stare right at God's creatures as if embracing the whole world with eyes of tenderness. Everyone was in love with her but she had eyes for no one but Sayyid Abu Ghaneema, the one who owned the date palms on the borders of the village towards the mountain. Tall and broad he was like a piece of rock torn out of the mountain side; his heart was like steel and he feared neither djinn nor wolf. But when of an afternoon he would be dangling hook and line from the canal bank and he would meet her, his ruddy face would turn pale and he would lower his head. Giving that laugh of hers, she would stride off proudly. One day the wife was joking with her and the girl told her about herself and that night the wife related the story to me. In the morning I

49

called for him and said:

' "Sayyid my son, strive for what is legal."

' "The moon's too high up in the sky," he said to me, "and what's going to make it hang on the wall?"

' "You helpless boy," I said to him, "there's a proverb that says: 'Better a man's shade than a wall's shade.' Though your pocket is empty mine can look after all her demands."

'The fellow was delighted and went off with hope in his heart, and when the wife asked Mansoura about her conditions she said:

' "Auntie, I'm at the man's disposal. Sayyid's the best of men and so strong he'd tear down a mountain."

'And so trilling cries of joy rang out and a wedding party was held and the lucky man's hut became filled with lawful plenty, for people's hearts are filled with faith and generosity. The two of them bathed in the honey of happiness after the dark night of misery.'

Dahshan scratched his neck and shoved his skull-cap over his forehead.

'It's true, man,' he said – 'it's all a matter of luck.'

'But the lifespan of happiness is short, my son,' said the Sheikh, ' – as short as the life of a flower. The Devil went after them till he sowed mischief between them.'

The Sheikh fell silent and took several sips of tea. Meanwhile Dahshan had moved across towards the Sheikh and settled himself beside him on the grass.

'For the sake of the Prophet,' he said, 'tell us the rest of the story of Mansoura, Uncle.'

The Sheikh straightened himself and sat back on his heels. He rapped his hands against his knees.

'Why turn over what's buried and done with, my son?' he said. 'I don't like talking about the honour of women.'

'Man, tell us – does anything stay hidden?'

Said the Sheikh:

'When the watchman Hindawi was appointed in charge of the canal lock for the night shift, he went to Sayyid in his hut among the date palms by the mountain and said to him:

' "Date palms don't give much and you've got to be on your toes to earn a living. Mansoura's a nice girl and she deserves the best. With a bit of the sweat of your brow you could spare her doing the rounds from house to house with the water jar, her torn *galabia* all wet when the cold is at its worst. The season for the dates to ripen is still far off, so come and guard the beans I've planted in my field and I'll give you a quarter of the crop."

'Sayyid was delighted and would spend the night on Hindawi's land, tilling it in the early hours and sleeping like the dead and leaving Mansoura on her own by night in the hut – and the nights of winter know no end. He'd go off from here with his hoe and Hindawi would come knocking at the door from there, bringing with him sweets and things that dazzle a woman's eyes. The girl would open the door to him and she'd make him tea.'

'Ah, the vile, cunning fellow! And did he get the better of her, Sheikh Zeidan?'

'The Lord has ordered us to be discreet about such matters, my son. Allah alone knows whether she gave in to him – women aren't to be trusted – or whether perhaps he took her by force and the poor girl kept quiet about it, for such as her are weak and vulnerable. Whatever it was, he used to stay on and wouldn't go on his way till dawn, before Sayyid's return. Walls have ears, though, and the story got about and lewd songs came out about her, and the strange thing is that Sayyid would sing them and laugh as he was hoeing Hindawi's land with the sweat of his brow and watching over it, without knowing that the words were talking of his own honour.

'After Sayyid had brought in the crop of beans and had taken his share and stored it away in his hut, Mansoura got him to swear he'd not leave her on her own again, so he went off to Hindawi and said to him:

' "I've had enough, man – Mansoura's frightened of the mountain wolves and wants me to stay by her."

'Hindawi ground his teeth in rage and kept silent. The fire of love had taken flame in his heart, and Mansoura had become for him like a drug. He comforted himself with the thought of the proverb that says "Hunger's an infidel", and that tomorrow Sayyid would be back like a dog. Every time, though, Sayyid thought about it Mansoura would implore him not to leave her alone.'

'And then what happened, Sheikh Zeidan?' said one of the men, feeding the fire with more wood, as he saw the Sheikh seemingly reluctant to continue.

'When I returned at the end of the summer,' Sheikh Zeidan went on, 'Mansoura had completely disappeared. They said that Sayyid was like someone who's lost his reason. He searched everywhere for her – in the fields, up in the mountains, everywhere. Everyone asked about her but no one knew where she'd gone. Some said the mountain wolves had got her, others that Sayyid had learnt what had happened and had killed her.

'Then one day, at the first light of dawn, Hindawi was standing guard when he spotted something all swollen and bloated being held back by the lock gates, something blue like the carcase of some animal thrown into the canal, being tossed about to right and left by the waves. When he looked carefully at the raised, swollen arm in which were buried rusty bangles, he knew it was Mansoura. When they brought in the body they saw that Sayyid couldn't bring himself to look at her. Instead he kept looking at Hindawi and saying nothing. At last, when they accused him of murdering her, he confessed. "Only blood," he said, "washes dishonour clean." So they put him in irons and the judge gave him three years.'

Dahshan wiped the sweat from his neck and exclaimed:

'Poor fellow! By Allah, if I'd been the judge I'd have let him off. After all, what choice did he have? Only blood washes dishonour clean.'

'My son,' said the Sheikh, 'Sayyid didn't kill her or do anything of the sort. Pride made him confess so that later he could take his revenge on the real murderer.'

'Hindawi?' suggested Dahshan.

'Who else?' said the Sheikh. 'No sooner had they taken Sayyid away to prison than Hindawi broke down completely. He would wander round the village calling out her name and crying like a small child that's lost its mother. Then one night he came to me and said he couldn't go on living in the village, that Mansoura's image, with her swollen arm and the rusty bangles, was always in front of him. He then told me the real story of what had happened to Mansoura. It seems that when Sayyid gave up working for Hindawi and was with Mansoura all the time, Hindawi was eaten up with love and jealousy. He just couldn't live without her. Then one day he came across her when she was alone, filling her water jar from the canal. He asked her to find a way of being with him again, of leaving Sayyid if necessary and marrying him. She told him that what had been between them was past and done with, that she belonged to Sayyid. Blinded by desire and jealousy, he attacked her, hoping to have his way with her and to bring her back to him. It seems she slipped in the mud and fell into the canal and in a matter of seconds she'd been swallowed up by the waves and it wasn't till days later that Hindawi found her body way down by the lock. "How could I kill Mansoura?" Hindawi had said to me in a voice choked with tears. "How could I kill someone who was dearer to me than life?" Anyway, Hindawi was frightened that when he came out of prison Sayyid would take his revenge of him. He therefore asked me to take him to work with me in Cairo.'

Dahshan looked round at the faces of the men in alarm.

'Don't worry, my boy,' Sheikh Zeidan assured him. 'Hindawi's no longer of this world – it was Mansoura who took her revenge of him.'

'How can the dead take revenge?' muttered Dahshan.

'I told you Mansoura had special powers,' Sheikh Zeidan answered him. 'It happened like this: I brought Hindawi and he joined up with us. Then one day – may you not see its like, my son – we were working just as we were doing today – the Lord of the Kaaba and these men are my witnesses – and Hindawi and I were in the trench and the bulldozer came up with another length of pipe. I saw Hindawi's eyes as he looked up at it, his hands held out to take hold of it. There was terror in his eyes as if he'd seen a ghost and the next moment, just as if a secret hand had loosened the cables round it, the pipe fell full on Hindawi. We managed to shift the pipe from on top of him but there was no hope. Just before he died he looked up at the bulldozer. Perhaps for him the arm of the bulldozer had become the swollen arm of Mansoura with the rusted bangles. Anyway, the only words he uttered before he died were: "Mansoura, you cruel one." '

Sheikh Zeidan turned to Dahshan. 'So you see, my boy, why it is that we always call upon Mansoura to make the work easier for us. Mansoura, my son, has special powers.'

Sheikh Zeidan stared out silently at the bulldozer crouched in the semi-darkness like some beast of burden taking its nightly rest. Then he yawned and stretched and rose to his feet.

'It's an early start tomorrow, men, and we'd better get some sleep.'

He walked off into the darkness and, raising his *galabia*, made water against the bole of a casuarina tree, then washed at the tap and entered the tent.

The Long Night of Winter

ᴗᴗᴗᴗᴗᴗᴗᴗᴗᴗᴗᴗᴗᴗᴗᴗᴗᴗᴗᴗᴗᴗᴗᴗᴗᴗᴗᴗᴗᴗᴗᴗᴗᴗᴗᴗ

In an instant between sleep and wakefulness, an instant outside the bounds of time, that gave the sensation of being eternal, the sounds of night, like slippery fishes passing through the mesh of a net, registered themselves on Zennouba's hearing, filtering gradually into her awakening consciousness: the machine-like croaking of frogs, and the barking of dogs in the fields answered by the dogs of the village on the other bank in a never-ending exchange of information in some code language.

All at once she realized that she was in bed and that she was alone. The only other live things in the room were the leaping shapes on the peeling wall made by the dying wick in the kerosene lamp that looked down from the small aperture. She knew with certainty that she would now sleep no longer that night, and she longed for the day to come with the call to dawn prayers.

As she waited for the return of her husband, memories of the past took over from the sounds of night, and as on many such a night she guided herself back to the days of her childhood, to that closed society that children effortlessly set up for themselves, days of security in a house where love and tenderness were a child's right and did not have to be earned, where death was without dominion and sorrow never lasted beyond a night. She would play in the lanes of the village with her friends, coming and going as she pleased, and sometimes, on moonlit nights, she would walk in the fields with a group of young girls, singing songs charged with meanings that she only vaguely and deliciously understood, songs like: 'The winter's night is long. Hug me and I'll hug you in the long winter's night', which they sang over and over again tirelessly, clapping their hands to its rhythm. Then, suddenly, with puberty pushing her sprouting breasts against the rough calico of her *galabia*, she was torn, like a foetus from the womb's warmth, out of her world of childish freedom and prevented from playing with her companions. Soon afterwards she was married to her cousin, Hagg Hamdan, so that the land might stay in the family, and she moved from her home among the closely-packed village houses to the lonely mansion that lay on her husband's lands on the other bank, with its two high storeys and the north-facing reception rooms paved with stone, and the winter rooms with their wooden floors, and its fruit and vegetable gardens, the whole surrounded by a high mud wall topped by pieces of broken glass. She particularly remembers, on her wedding day when they first took her through the wide gateway, the large camel painted in red against the white-washed wall, symbolizing the owner's pilgrimage, and the red palms of hands to ward off the evil eye.

And so had come the night when Hagg Hamdan had taken her to this same bed. It had been a night of violence and pain, utterly unrelated to any previous experience she had had. Since then it had been repeated hundreds of times, with the element of pain replaced by that of repugnance at the rough hands that kneaded her body, and the evil-smelling breath and spittle of a *habitué* of the blue smoke of hashish. In compliance to her husband, and for the sake of the children, she had submitted to the role of wife and mother, a woman protected by marriage and by the home that she would leave only when they bore her to her grave.

She recalled the first night she had woken to find that he was no longer beside her, and how she had got up to look for him and had found him lying on the stone bench above the oven with the young servant girl. When he had returned with her to their room, her hatred and bitterness had been so great that, contrary to all teachings and traditions, she had demanded a divorce. He had turned his back on her, saying: 'Why should I divorce you? Why don't you go and ask your mother about your father who spent so much of his time on his prayer mat? Go to sleep and let's not have any more trouble.' The following day he had brought her a pair of gold earrings and had kissed her head affectionately. Yet, with the passing of time, such nights were repeated and gifts of gold jewellery were made to her, while the girl servants came and went at his bidding without apparent reason, for he was the master of the house.

The doubts concerning her father, born of her husband's remark on that fateful night, continued to assail her. Could there be any truth in the insinuation about the dignified and pious man who had such influence in the village, that man with the kindly, bearded face who would sometimes take her on his knee and tell her stories from the Qur'an about the prophets, then, when he thought she had fallen to sleep, would carry her to bed? The mere touch of his *aba*, with its heavy smell of musk as she buried her face in its folds, gave her comfort and assurance that her father was good and that all was well with the world.

She re-enacted to herself that morning when her mother had visited her, coming from the village and crossing the bridge on a donkey and accompanied by a servant laden down with baskets of pies and pastries. It was on the morning of the eve of the Feast and the old lady had been to visit her husband's grave in the cemetery and had then completed her journey to her daughter's house. Between sips of tea her mother poured out the news of the village. At last Zennouba took courage and asked the question that had been in her mind for so long. Her mother lowered her gaze to the glass of tea in her hand and said:

'All men are like that.'

'Even my father?'

The mother sipped noisily at her tea before answering:

'Daughter, he too was a man. Allah have mercy on him and show him His favours.'

She would have liked to draw her mother out further. Had her mother suffered the same sort of nightmare of a life as she did? Was this the fate of all women? Her mother, though, had given her a glance that had silenced her, a warning not to tread on forbidden territory. Then her mother had broken into a recital of the Fatiha for the soul of her husband and Zennouba had repeated the words after her. Now her mother too was dead.

Zennouba's husband had reached the same age as her father when he had died, and his joints creaked and cracked as he prayed. Even so, he would still disappear of nights and she would still receive presents of jewellery from him. Surely there must come a time when he had had his fill? For a short time, she thought that he had at last changed. Then, suddenly, the girl servant had started to become insolent, to refuse to accept her orders, and she knew the reason instinctively. Her hopes frustrated, she had at last asserted herself and insisted that the girl be sent back to her village, and only a few days ago another one, little more than a child, had been brought to the house and had spent her first two days crying for her mother. Where else could he now be except with her? Was it possible?

As she stared at the glow from the dying coals in the earthenware fire at the foot of the bed, undecided whether to rise and go downstairs, she heard his hesitant, shuffling footsteps, and closed her eyes. He lay down quietly beside her, drew the covering over himself and almost immediately fell asleep.

She moved slightly in the bed, avoiding him, her own body tense. The pent-up hatred against him had long ago changed to a cold contempt; the hopes that things would change had now gone, but the ache to love and be loved was still there, as physically part of her as her sight or sense of smell. The lamp spluttered and she looked up at the small aperture and saw the first greyness of dawn seeping into the room. Holding her breath, she sidled off the bed and made her way, hands outstretched before her, out of the room, then, finding the bannisters, went downstairs to where the girl slept over the oven.

Nargis raised her head.

'Nothing wrong, lady Zennouba?'

'Nothing, Nargis,' she said. 'Nothing at all. Get up and bring hot water – I want a bath.'

She returned to the room. Her husband was still fast asleep. Collecting up her towel, also the earthenware fire, she went out to the bathroom. She put down the fire and blew at the coals, bringing them to life, then took down the oval tin basin that was leaning against the wall.

Nargis came carrying a large jug of hot water to which she had added some drops of rose water. Zennouba took off her nightrobe and stepped into the basin. As she looked at Nargis, the other turned her face away.

'Don't be afraid, Nargis,' she said. 'Take off your nightdress so you can wash my back.'

Turning round, Nargis drew her dress over her head, then faced her mistress. Zennouba looked at the girl's body and the thought occurred to her that she too had once been as beautiful. She was about to say so to the girl, then decided against it. Instead she said:

'I hope you'll be happy here, Nargis. God willing, you'll stay a long time in this house.' Then she squatted down in the basin so that the girl would pour the water over her back.

'Scrub my back with the loofah,' she said, and as the girl leant over her, Zennouba was aware of the taut breasts brushing against her shoulder.

'Scrub harder,' she said. 'Harder, harder.' And the rough loofah scraped painfully across her back.

My World of the Unknown

~~~~~~

There are many mysteries in life, unseen powers in the universe, worlds other than our own, hidden links and radiations that draw creatures together and whose effect is interacting. They may merge or be incompatible, and perhaps the day will come when science will find a method for connecting up these worlds in the same way as it has made it possible to voyage to other planets. Who knows?

Yet one of these other worlds I have explored; I have lived in it and been linked with its creatures through the bond of love. I used to pass with amazing speed between this tangible world of ours and another invisible earth, mixing in the two worlds on one and the same day, as though living it twice over.

When entering into the world of my love, and being summoned and yielding to its call, no one around me would be aware of what was happening to me. All that occurred was that I would be overcome by something resembling a state of languor and would go off into a semi-sleep. Nothing about me would change except that I would become very silent and withdrawn, though I am normally a person who is talkative and eager to go out into the world of people. I would yearn to be on my own, would long for the moment of surrender as I prepared myself for answering the call.

Love had its beginning when an order came through for my husband to be transferred to a quiet country town and, being too busy with his work, delegated to me the task of going to this town to choose suitable accommodation prior to his taking up the new appointment. He cabled one of his subordinates named Kamil and asked him to meet me at the station and to assist me.

I took the early morning train. The images of a dream I had had that night came to me as I looked out at the vast fields and gauged the distances between the towns through which the train passed and reckoned how far it was between the new town in which we were fated to live and beloved Cairo.

The images of the dream kept reappearing to me, forcing themselves upon my mind: images of a small white house surrounded by a garden with bushes bearing yellow flowers, a house lying on the edge of a broad canal in which were swans and tall sailing boats. I kept on wondering at my dream and trying to analyse it. Perhaps it was some secret wish I had had, or maybe the echo of some image that my unconscious had stored up and was chewing over.

As the train arrived at its destination, I awoke from my thoughts. I found Kamil awaiting me. We set out in his car, passing through the local *souk*. I gazed at the mounds of fruit with delight, chatting away happily with Kamil. When we emerged from the *souk* we found ourselves on the bank of the Mansoura canal, a canal on which swans swam and sailing boats moved to and fro. I kept staring at them with uneasy longing. Kamil directed the driver to the residential buildings the governorate had put up for housing government employees. While gazing at the opposite bank a large boat with a great fluttering sail glided past. Behind it could be seen a white house that had a garden with trees with yellow flowers and that lay on its own amidst vast fields. I shouted out in confusion, overcome by the feeling that I had been here before.

'Go to that house,' I called to the driver. Kamil leapt up, objecting vehemently: 'No, no, – no one lives in that house. The best thing is to go to the employees' buildings.'

I shouted insistently, like someone hypnotized: 'I must have a look at that house.' 'All right,' he said. 'You won't like it, though – it's old and needs repairing.' Giving in to my wish, he ordered the driver to make his way there.

At the garden door we found a young woman, spare and of fair complexion. A fat child with ragged clothes encircled her neck with his burly legs. In a strange silence, she stood as though nailed to the ground, barring the door with her hands and looking at us with doltish enquiry.

I took a sweet from my bag and handed it to the boy. He snatched it eagerly, tightening his grip on her neck with his podgy, mud-bespattered feet so that her face became flushed from his high-spirited embrace. A half-smile showed on her tightly-closed lips. Taking courage, I addressed her in a friendly tone: 'I'd like to see over this house.' She braced her hands resolutely against the door. 'No,' she said quite simply. I turned helplessly to Kamil, who went up to her and pushed her violently in the chest so that she staggered back. 'Don't you realize,' he shouted at her, 'that this is the director's wife? Off with you!'

Lowering her head so that the child all but slipped from her, she walked off dejectedly to the canal bank where she lay down on the ground, put the child on her lap, and rested her head in her hands in silent submission.

Moved by pity, I remonstrated: 'There's no reason to be so rough, Mr Kamil. Who is the woman?' 'Some mad woman,' he said with a shrug of his shoulders, 'who's a stranger to the town. Out of kindness the owner of this house put her in charge of it until someone should come along to live in it.'

With increased interest I said: 'Will he be asking a high rent for it?' 'Not at all,' he said with an enigmatic smile. 'He'd welcome anyone taking it over. There are no restrictions and the rent is modest – no more than four pounds.'

I was beside myself with joy. Who in these days can find somewhere to live for such an amount? I rushed through the door into the house with Kamil behind me and went over the rooms: five spacious rooms with wooden floors, with a pleasant hall, modern lavatory, and a beautifully roomy kitchen with a large verandah overlooking vast pistachio-green fields of generously watered rice. A breeze, limpid and cool, blew, playing with the tips of the crop and making the delicate leaves move in continuous dancing waves.

I went back to the first room with its spacious balcony overlooking the road and revealing the other bank of the canal where, along its strand, extended the houses of the town. Kamil pointed out to me a building facing the house on the other side. 'That's where we work,' he said, 'and behind it is where the children's schools are.'

'Thanks be to God,' I said joyfully. 'It means that everything is within easy reach of this house – and the *souk*'s nearby too.' 'Yes,' he said, 'and the fishermen will knock at your door to show you the fresh fish they've caught in their nets. But the house needs painting and re-doing, also there are all sorts of rumours about it – the people around here believe in djinn and spirits.'

'This house is going to be my home,' I said with determination. 'Its low rent will make up for whatever we may have to spend on re-doing it. You'll see what this house will look like when I get the garden arranged. As for the story about djinn and spirits, just leave them to us – we're more spirited than them.'

We laughed at my joke as we left the house. On my way to the station we agreed about the repairs that needed doing to the house. Directly I reached Cairo I cabled my husband to send the furniture from the town we had been living in, specifying a suitable date to fit in with the completion of the repairs and the house being ready for occupation.

On the date fixed I once again set off and found that all my wishes had been carried out and that the house was pleasantly spruce with its rooms painted a cheerful orange tinge, the floors well polished and the garden tidied up and made into small flowerbeds.

I took possession of the keys and Kamil went off to attend to his business, having put a chair on the front balcony for me to sit on while I awaited the arrival of the furniture van. I stretched out contentedly in the chair and gazed at the two banks with their towering trees like two rows of guards between which passed the boats with their lofty sails, while around them glided a male swan heading a flotilla of females. Halfway across the canal he turned and flirted with them, one after the other, like a sultan amidst his harem.

Relaxed, I closed my eyes. I projected myself into the future and pictured to myself the enjoyment I would have in this house after it had been put in order and the garden fixed up. I awoke to the touch of clammy fingers shaking me by the shoulders.

I started and found myself staring at the fair-complexioned woman with her child squatting on her shoulders as she stood erect in front of me staring at me in silence. 'What do you want?' I said to her sharply. 'How did you get in?' 'I got in with this,' she said simply, revealing a key between her fingers.

I snatched the key from her hand as I loudly rebuked her: 'Give it here. We have rented the house and you have no right to come into it like this.' 'I have a lot of other keys,' she answered briefly. 'And what,' I said to her, 'do you want of this house?' 'I want to stay on in it and for you to go,' she said. I laughed in amazement at her words as I asked myself: Is she really mad? Finally I said impatiently: 'Listen here, I'm not leaving here and you're not entering this house unless I wish it. My husband is coming with the children, and the furniture is on the way. He'll be arriving in a little while and we'll be living here for such period of time as my husband is required to work in this town.'

She looked at me in a daze. For a long time she was silent, then she said: 'All right, your husband will stay with me and you can go.' Despite my utter astonishment I felt pity for her. 'I'll allow you to stay on with us for the little boy's sake,' I said to her gently, 'until you find yourself another place. If you'd like to help me with the housework I'll pay you what you ask.'

Shaking her head, she said with strange emphasis: 'I'm not a servant. I'm Aneesa.' 'You're not staying here,' I said to her coldly, rising to my feet. Collecting all my courage and emulating Kamil's determination when he rebuked her, I began pushing her in the chest as I caught hold of the young boy's hand. 'Get out of here and don't come near this house,' I shouted at her. 'Let me have all the keys. I'll not let go of your child till you've given them all to me.'

With a set face that did not flicker she put her hand to her bosom and took out a ring on which were several keys, which she dropped into my hand. I released my grip on the young boy. Supporting him on her shoulders, she started to leave. Regretting my harshness, I took out several piastres from my bag and placed them in the boy's hand. With the same silence and stiffness she wrested the piastres from the boy's hand and gave them back to me. Then she went straight out. Bolting the door this time, I sat down, tense and upset, to wait.

My husband arrived, then the furniture, and for several days I occupied myself with putting the house in order. My husband was busy with his work and the children occupied themselves with making new friends and I completely forgot about Aneesa, that is until my husband returned one night wringing his hands with fury: 'This woman Aneesa, can you imagine that since we came to live in this house she's been hanging around it every night. Tonight she was so crazy she blocked my way and suggested I should send you off so that she might live with me. The woman's gone completely off her head about this house and I'm afraid she might do something to the children or assault you.'

Joking with him and masking the jealousy that raged within me, I said: 'And what is there for you to get angry about? She's a fair and attractive enough woman – a blessing brought to your very doorstep!' With a sneer he took up the telephone, muttering: 'May God look after her!'

He contacted the police and asked them to come and take her away. When I heard the sound of the police van coming I ran to the window and saw them taking her off. The poor woman did not resist, did not object, but submitted with a gentle sadness that as usual with her aroused one's pity. Yet, when she saw me standing in tears and watching her, she turned to me and, pointing to the wall of the house, called out: 'I'll leave her to you.' 'Who?' I shouted. 'Who, Aneesa?' Once again pointing at the bottom of the house, she said: 'Her.'

The van took her off and I spent a sleepless night. No sooner did day come than I hurried to the garden to examine my plants and to walk round the house and carefully inspect its walls. All I found were some cracks, the house being old, and I laughed at the frivolous thought that came to me: Could, for example, there be jewels buried here, as told in fairy tales?

Who could 'she' be? What was the secret of this house? Who was Aneesa and was she really mad? Where were she and her son living? So great did my concern for Aneesa become that I began pressing my husband with questions until he brought me news of her. The police had learnt that she was the wife of a well-to-do teacher living in a nearby town. One night he had caught her in an act of infidelity, and in fear she had fled with her son and had settled here, no one knowing why she had betaken herself to this particular house. However, the owner of the house had been good enough to allow her to put up in it until someone should come to live in it, while some kind person had intervened on her behalf to have her name included among those receiving monthly allowances from the Ministry of Social Affairs. There were many rumours that cast doubt upon her conduct: people passing by her house at night would hear her conversing with unknown persons. Her madness took the form of a predilection for silence and isolation from people during the daytime as she wandered about in a dream world. After the police had persuaded them to take her in to safeguard the good repute of her family, she was returned to her relatives.

The days passed and the story of Aneesa was lost in oblivion. Winter came and with it heavy downpours of rain. The vegetation in my garden flourished though the castor-oil plants withered and their yellow flowers fell. I came to find pleasure in sitting out on the kitchen balcony looking at my flowers and vegetables and enjoying the belts of sunbeams that lay between the clouds and lavished my balcony with warmth and light.

One sunny morning my attention was drawn to the limb of a nearby tree whose branches curved up gracefully despite its having dried up and its dark bark being cracked. My gaze was attracted by something twisting and turning along the tip of a branch: bands of yellow and others of red, intermingled with bands of black, were creeping forward. It was a long, smooth tube, at its end a small striped head with two bright, wary eyes.

The snake curled round on itself in spiral rings, then tautened its body and moved forward. The sight gripped me; I felt terror turning my blood cold and freezing my limbs.

My senses were numbed, my soul intoxicated with a strange elation at the exciting beauty of the snake. I was rooted to the spot, wavering between two thoughts that contended in my mind at one and the same time: should I snatch up some implement from the kitchen and kill the snake, or should I enjoy the rare moment of beauty that had been afforded me?

As though the snake had read what was passing through my mind, it raised its head, tilting it to right and left in thrilling coquetry. Then, by means of two tiny fangs like pearls, and a golden tongue like a twig of *arak* wood, it smiled at me and fastened its eyes on mine in one fleeting, commanding glance. The thought of killing left me. I felt a current, a radiation from its eyes that penetrated to my heart ordering me to stay where I was. A warning against continuing to sit out there in front of it surged inside me, but my attraction to it paralysed my limbs and I did not move. I kept on watching it, utterly entranced and captivated. Like a bashful virgin being lavished with compliments, it tried to conceal its pride in its beauty, and, having made certain of captivating its lover, the snake coyly twisted round and gently, gracefully glided away until swallowed up by a crack in the wall. Could the snake be the 'she' that Aneesa had referred to on the day of her departure?

At last I rose from my place, overwhelmed by the feeling that I was on the brink of a new world, a new destiny, or rather, if you wish, the threshold of a new love. I threw myself onto the bed in a dreamlike state, unaware of the passage of time. No sooner, though, did I hear my husband's voice and the children with their clatter as they returned at noon than I regained my sense of being a human being, wary and frightened about itself, determined about the existence and continuance of its species. Without intending to I called out: 'A snake – there's a snake in the house.'

My husband took up the telephone and some men came and searched the house. I pointed out to them the crack into which the snake had disappeared, though racked with a feeling of remorse at being guilty of betrayal. For here I was denouncing the beloved, inviting people against it after it had felt safe with me.

The men found no trace of the snake. They burned some wormwood and fumigated the hole but without result. Then my husband summoned Sheikh Farid, Sheikh of the Rifa'iyya order in the town, who went on chanting verses from the Qur'an as he tapped the ground with his stick. He then asked to speak to me alone and said:

'Madam, the sovereign of the house has sought you out and what you saw is no snake, rather it is one of the monarchs of the earth – may God make your words pleasant to them – who has appeared to you in the form of a snake. Here in this house there are many holes of snakes, but they are of the non-poisonous kind. They inhabit houses and go and come as they please. What you saw, though, is something else.'

'I don't believe a word of it,' I said, stupefied. 'This is nonsense. I know that the djinn are creatures that actually exist, but they are not in touch with our world, there is no contact between them and the world of humans.'

With an enigmatic smile he said: 'My child, the Prophet went out to them and read the Qur'an to them in their country. Some of them are virtuous and some of them are Muslims, and how do you know there is no contact between us and them? Let your prayer be "O Lord, increase me in knowledge" and do not be nervous. Your purity of spirit, your translucence of soul have opened to you doors that will take you to other worlds known only to their Creator. Do not be afraid. Even if you should find her one night sleeping in your bed, do not be alarmed but talk to her with all politeness and friendliness.'

'That's enough of all that, Sheikh Farid. Thank you,' I said, alarmed, and he left us.

We went on discussing the matter. 'Let's be practical,' suggested my husband, 'and stop all the cracks at the bottom of the outside walls and put wire-mesh over the windows, also paint wormwood all round the garden fence.'

We set about putting into effect what we had agreed. I, though, no longer dared to go out onto the balconies. I neglected my garden and stopped wandering about in it. Generally I would spend my free time in bed. I changed to being someone who liked to sit around lazily and was disinclined to mix with people; those diversions and recreations that previously used to tempt me no longer gave me any pleasure. All I wanted was to stretch myself out and drowse. In bewilderment I asked myself: Could it be that I was in love? But how could I love a snake? Or could she really be one of the daughters of the monarchs of the djinn? I would awake from my musings to find that I had been wandering in my thoughts and recalling to mind how magnificent she was. And what is the secret of her beauty? I would ask myself. Was it that I was fascinated by her multi-coloured, supple body? Or was it that I had been dazzled by that intelligent, commanding way she had of looking at me? Or could it be the sleek way she had of gliding along, so excitingly dangerous, that had captivated me?

Excitingly dangerous! No doubt it was this excitement that had stirred my feelings and awakened my love, for did they not make films to excite and frighten? There was no doubt but that the secret of my passion for her, my preoccupation with her, was due to the excitement that had aroused, through intense fear, desire within myself; an excitement that was sufficiently strong to drive the blood hotly through my veins whenever the memory of her came to me, thrusting the blood in bursts that made my heart beat wildly, my limbs limp. And so, throwing myself down in a pleasurable state of torpor, my craving for her would be awakened and I would wish for her coil-like touch, her graceful gliding motion.

And yet I fell to wondering how union could come about, how craving be quenched, the delights of the body be realized, between a woman and a snake. And did she, I wondered, love me and want me as I loved her? An idea would obtrude itself upon me sometimes: did Cleopatra, the very legend of love, have sexual intercourse with her serpent after having given up sleeping with men, having wearied of amorous adventures with them so that her sated instincts were no longer moved other than by the excitement of fear, her senses no longer aroused other than by bites from a snake? And the last of her lovers had been a viper that had destroyed her.

I came to live in a state of continuous torment, for a strange feeling of longing scorched my body and rent my senses, while my circumstances obliged me to carry out the duties and responsibilities that had been placed on me as the wife of a man who occupied an important position in the small town, he and his family being objects of attention and his house a Kaaba for those seeking favours; also as a mother who must look after her children and concern herself with every detail of their lives so as to exercise control over them; there was also the house and its chores, this house that was inhabited by the mysterious lover who lived in a world other than mine. How, I wondered, was union between us to be achieved? Was wishing for this love a sin or was there nothing to reproach myself about?

And as my self-questioning increased so did my yearning, my curiosity, my desire. Was the snake from the world of reptiles or from the djinn? When would the meeting be? Was she, I wondered, aware of me and would she return out of pity for my consuming passion?

One stormy morning with the rain pouring down so hard that I could hear the drops rattling on the window pane, I lit the stove and lay down in bed between the covers seeking refuge from an agonizing trembling that racked my yearning body which, ablaze with unquenchable desire, called out for relief.

I heard a faint rustling sound coming from the corner of the wall right beside my bed. I looked down and kept my eyes fixed on one of the holes in the wall, which I found was slowly, very slowly, expanding. Closing my eyes, my heart raced with joy and my body throbbed with mounting desire as there dawned in me the hope of an encounter. I lay back in submission to what was to be. No longer did I care whether love was coming from the world of reptiles or from that of the djinn, sovereigns of the world. Even were this love to mean my destruction, my desire for it was greater.

I heard a hissing noise that drew nearer, then it changed to a gentle whispering in my ear, calling to me: 'I am love, O enchantress. I showed you my home in your sleep; I called to you to my kingdom when your soul was dozing on the horizon of dreams, so come, my sweet beloved, come and let us explore the depths of the azure sea of pleasure. There, in the chamber of coral, amidst cool, shady rocks where reigns deep, restful silence lies our bed, lined with soft, bright green damask, inlaid with pearls newly wrenched from their shells. Come, let me sleep with you as I have slept with beautiful women and have given them bliss. Come, let me prise out your pearl from its shell that I may polish it and bring forth its splendour. Come to where no one will find us, where no one will see us, for the eyes of swimming creatures are innocent and will not heed what we do nor understand what we say. Down there lies repose, lies a cure for all your yearnings and ills. Come, without fear or dread, for no creature will reach us in our hidden world, and only the eye of God alone will see us; He alone will know what we are about and He will watch over us.'

I began to be intoxicated by the soft musical whisperings. I felt her cool and soft and smooth, her coldness producing a painful convulsion in my body and hurting me to the point of terror. I felt her as she slipped between the covers, then her two tiny fangs, like two pearls, began to caress my body; arriving at my thighs, the golden tongue, like an *arak* twig, inserted its pronged tip between them and began sipping and exhaling; sipping the poisons of my desire and exhaling the nectar of my ecstasy, till my whole body tingled and started to shake in sharp, painful, rapturous spasms – and all the while the tenderest of words were whispered to me as I confided to her all my longings.

At last the cool touch withdrew, leaving me exhausted. I went into a deep slumber to awake at noon full of energy, all of me a joyful burgeoning to life. Curiosity and a desire to know who it was seized me again. I looked at the corner of the wall and found that the hole was wide open. Once again I was overcome by fear. I pointed out the crack to my husband, unable to utter, although terror had once again awakened in me passionate desire. My husband filled up the crack with cement and went to sleep.

Morning came and everyone went out. I finished my housework and began roaming around the rooms in boredom, battling against the desire to surrender myself to sleep. I sat in the hallway and suddenly she appeared before me, gentle as an angel, white as day, softly undulating and flexing herself, calling to me in her bewitching whisper: 'Bride of mine, I called you and brought you to my home. I have wedded you, so there is no sin in our love, nothing to reproach yourself about. I am the guardian of the house, and I hold sway over the snakes and vipers that inhabit it, so come and I shall show you where they live. Have no fear so long as we are together. You and I are in accord. Bring a container with water and I shall place my fingers over your hand and we shall recite together some verses from the Qur'an, then we shall sprinkle it in the places from which they emerge and shall thus close the doors on them, and it shall be a pact between us that your hands will not do harm to them.'

'Then you are one of the monarchs of the djinn?' I asked eagerly.

'Why do you not bring me treasures and riches as we hear about in fables when a human takes as sister her companion among the djinn?'

She laughed at my words, shaking her golden hair that was like dazzling threads of light. She whispered to me, coquettishly: 'How greedy is mankind! Are not the pleasures of the body enough? Were I to come to you with wealth we would both die consumed by fire.'

'No, no,' I called out in alarm. 'God forbid that I should ask for unlawful wealth. I merely asked it of you as a test, that it might be positive proof that I am not imagining things and living in dreams.'

She said: 'And do intelligent humans have to have something tangible as evidence? By God, do you not believe in His ability to create worlds and living beings? Do you not know that you have an existence in worlds other than that of matter and the transitory? Fine, since you ask for proof, come close to me and my caresses will put vitality back into your limbs. You will retain your youth. I shall give you abiding youth and the delights of love – and they are more precious than wealth in the world of man. How many fortunes have women spent in quest of them? As for me I shall feed from the poisons of your desire, the exhalations of your burning passion, for that is my nourishment and through it I live.'

'I thought that your union with me was for love, not for nourishment and the perpetuation of youth and vigour,' I said in amazement.

'And is sex anything but food for the body and an interaction in union and love?' she said. 'Is it not this that makes human beings happy and is the secret of feeling joy and elation?'

She stretched out her radiant hand to my body, passing over it like the sun's rays and discharging into it warmth and a sensation of languor.

'I am ill,' I said. 'I am ill. I am ill,' I kept on repeating. When he heard me my husband brought the doctor, who said: 'High blood pressure, heart trouble, nervous depression.' Having prescribed

OTTAKAR'S
a love for books

The Edinburgh Bookshop
57 George Street
Edinburgh, EH2 2JG
0131 225 4495
george.street@ottakars.co.uk

SALE

27 3 83714   16 Aug 2004 17:37

CASHIER: ELLIE W

'80435909123 DISTANT VIEW OF   5.99

TOTAL   ITEMS   1   5.99

CASH   20.00
CHANGE CASH   14.01-

Head Office: St John's House,
72 St John's Road, London SW11 1PT

Vat No: 561997200
Company Reg No: 2133199

various medicaments he left. The stupidity of doctors! My doctor did not know that he was describing the symptoms of love, did not even know it was from love I was suffering. Yet I knew my illness and the secret of my cure. I showed my husband the enlarged hole in the wall and once again he stopped it up. We then carried the bed to another corner.

After some days had passed I found another hole alongside my bed. My beloved came and whispered to me: 'Why are you so coy and flee from me, my bride? Is it fear of your being rebuffed or is it from aversion? Are you not happy with our being together? Why do you want for us to be apart?'

'I am in agony,' I whispered back. 'Your love is so intense and the desire to enjoy you so consuming. I am frightened I shall feel that I am tumbling down into a bottomless pit and being destroyed.'

'My beloved,' she said. 'I shall only appear to you in beauty's most immaculate form.'

'But it is natural for you to be a man,' I said in a precipitate outburst, 'seeing that you are so determined to have a love affair with me.'

'Perfect beauty is to be found only in woman,' she said, 'so yield to me and I shall let you taste undreamed of happiness; I shall guide you to worlds possessed of such beauty as you have never imagined.'

She stretched out her fingers to caress me, while her delicate mouth sucked in the poisons of my desire and exhaled the nectar of my ecstasy, carrying me off into a trance of delicious happiness.

After that we began the most pleasurable of love affairs, wandering together in worlds and living on horizons of dazzling beauty, a world fashioned of jewels, a world whose every moment was radiant with light and formed a thousand shapes, a thousand colours.

As for the opening in the wall, I no longer took any notice. I no longer complained of feeling ill, in fact there burned within me abounding vitality. Sometimes I would bring a handful of wormwood and, by way of jest, would stop up the crack, just as the beloved teases her lover and closes the window in his face that, ablaze with desire for her, he may hasten to the door. After that I would sit for a long time and enjoy watching the wormwood powder being scattered in spiral rings by unseen puffs of wind. Then I would throw myself down on the bed and wait.

For months I immersed myself in my world, no longer calculating time or counting the days, until one morning my husband went out on the balcony lying behind our favoured wall alongside the bed. After a while I heard him utter a cry of alarm. We all hurried out to find him holding a stick, with a black, ugly snake almost two metres long, lying at his feet.

I cried out with a sorrow whose claws clutched at my heart so that it began to beat wildly. With crazed fury I shouted at my husband: 'Why have you broken the pact and killed it? What harm has it done?' How cruel is man! He lets no creature live in peace.

I spent the night sorrowful and apprehensive. My lover came to me and embraced me more passionately then ever. I whispered to her imploringly: 'Be kind, beloved. Are you angry with me or sad because of me?'

'It is farewell,' she said. 'You have broken the pact and have betrayed one of my subjects, so you must both depart from this house, for only love lives in it.'

In the morning I packed up so that we might move to one of the employees' buildings, leaving the house in which I had learnt of love and enjoyed incomparable pleasures.

I still live in memory and in hope. I crave for the house and miss my secret love. Who knows, perhaps one day my beloved will call me. Who really knows?

At the Time of the Jasmine

~~~~~~

He leaned his head against the backrest of the seat as the all-station train to Upper Egypt took him joltingly along, producing a doleful rhythm on the rails.

With his handkerchief he wiped his face, removing the specks of sand. Even so the view before his eyes remained blurred, the telegraph poles intermingling with the spectral forms of date palms that broke up into misty phantoms that were soon erased, leaving the yellow surface of sky to others which no sooner made their appearance than they vanished with the same speed.

He caught sight of some young boys plunging naked into the long winding cleft of the Ibrahimiyya Canal, cooling themselves in its shallow waters, while the sun's heat grew stronger, carrying with it what little breeze there was and turning it into a scorching inferno.

Time was at a standstill, stifling his breathing. He began toying wearily with his black tie as he glanced distractedly at the platforms of the small stations the train was passing by, amused at seeing the hefty men proudly clasping their guns slung on their shoulders, and the women spread out on the platform, their children carried close to them, while alongside them lay the cages of chickens they would be trading in the markets.

The cable he had received that morning lay in his jacket pocket.

'Your father Hagg Aballah Shalabi has died. Respect for the dead demands speedy burial.'

The words fell heavy as gravel in his throat, despite the fact that for a long time his father had, for him, been like someone already dead – ever since the day he had sent him away to the English school in Maadi some time after his mother's death.

Every morning his mother would place the silver ewer before him and he would rush off to where his father would be sitting at the edge of the prayer mat, his sleeves rolled up and his hands stretched out above the little silver basin and he would pour the water over them slowly and carefully, in his eyes an expression of admiration for his father as he made his ablutions; then he would pour the water over his feet from which he had removed his socks. He couldn't remember ever having opposed his father in anything, not even when he had carried him out to where the men were and had put him on Antar's back, laughing and boasting jubilantly:

'My son Hassan's a real man, a bold horseman – riding's in his blood.'

He hadn't been scared that day and hadn't looked up towards the window from which his mother surreptitiously gazed down on him, the kohl mixing in her eyes with tears of pity. He had merely let his short legs hang down the warm flanks and, taking the end of his *galabia* between his teeth, had clung with both hands to the long hair of the mane. Antar had rushed off with him, crossing the intersecting banked up tracks round the village, and had brought him back, prancing about amidst the admiring cries of the men.

Even when Muntaha, the sweet, shy girl with the thick black pigtails, had come to the house with her red box in her *howdah* on top of the camel from the neighbouring hamlet, and his father had carried her and put her into his bed where his mother used previously to sleep, even Muntaha he had loved. He would cling to her bright-coloured, scented dress as she went about the house, finding companionship in her from the loneliness he suffered after his mother had left him.

During the time away from home spent with foreign tutors his childhood quickly died, his love for his father froze and he himself became a sophisticated man not greatly concerned with emotions, subordinating everything to rational standards and to convention. The nostalgia within himself for his village Behbesheen was lost with the passing of the days, and the nights erased from his mind the memory of its rich pastures.

When he grew up he did his duty by visiting the place whenever his father was blessed with another child lest it be said of him that he was annoyed about brothers and sisters sharing with him his father's lands. Once he had opened his own accountancy office his visits grew less owing to his being taken up with business and then came to an end when he married his Turkish colleague Louga Hanem Toubchi. That day he had sent his father a cable reading: 'Am getting married tonight.'

His father received the news with silence, and when he was blessed with a daughter he again informed his father of the good news. The father contented himself by replying with a cable which said: 'Call her Jasmine.'

As the days passed his wife turned into a person who was always grumbling, afflicted by the arrogance of her countrymen. He bore her patiently until the day when she shouted at him:

'I am Louga Hanem Toubchi – is my name to become Madame Shalabi?'

'Go back to them,' he told her with frightening calm.

Taking her daughter, she had gone to the Toubchi household in Zamalek and he had stayed on in his flat in the centre of Cairo, not worried about being on his own. He let her be, thinking to break her obstinacy, but she only grew more stubborn and did not return. After this he did not think of visiting the village owing to his having become wrapped up in his work. Today, after the death of his father, his link with the rest of his relations would no doubt be cut and he would remain without roots.

The train stopped at Boush, his village's main township, so he took up his suitcase in which he had, together with his pyjamas, thrust the shroud he had bought before leaving Cairo. Duty demanded that he should bring with him a shroud that was in keeping with his father's position in the village. People would think badly of him if he didn't bring some white and green silk and a cashmere shawl and lay on a fine funeral night. In his pocket was a large sum he had drawn out from his savings at the bank to be spent on doing what was expected of him.

As he got down from the train he was seized by the hands of men come to convey their condolences. Faraghalli, who used as a child to steal with a fish hook the chickens of Madame Carmel, wife of the Health clerk, and who had now become a spokesman for the peasants, wrapped him round in an embrace inside his rich *aba* as he muttered:

'May God give you strength to bear this loss, Mr Hassan.'

He muttered some vague words in answer, then his hand was seized by the strong grasp of Sheikh Hammad, his father's overseer, as he passed him Antar's reins with the words:

'It's very hot, men, and it would be wrong of us to leave the dead man till midday.'

Hassan jumped onto Antar's back, proudly sitting upright in order to assure Sheikh Hammad that a soft hand had nothing to do with being a real man. The sun was sending down its scorching vertical shafts on to his bare head. The men were pressing their mounts forward, having let down the ends of their turbans to protect them from the blazing heat. He himself lifted up the morning newspaper over his head as he used to do in Cairo, then lowered it again to his side when he saw the line of girls from the jasmine factory standing and staring at him as he passed between them.

The blast of hot air brought with it the aroma of jasmine, whose pervasive smell clung to the flying specks of sand, penetrating deeply into men's chests so that, in time, all the people of the district suffered from a chronic cough – and no sooner had things quietened down than the next season had made its appearance.

By staying in Cairo he had escaped the malady but now, breathing in the aroma, he began to cough badly. With the coughing his eyes watered, until they became reddened and puffy, while Antar took him along the banked up tracks between the fields and then came to a stop in front of the stone wall surrounding the house.

'The burial permit is ready,' said Sheikh Hammad, 'and the sheikhs are here.'

As soon as he entered voices were raised in wailing from the women seated on the ground, who were covering their heads with earth.

His young brother came forward carrying the silver basin and ewer for him to make his ablutions, his face bearing the same dull dismay he himself had been afflicted with the day his mother had died.

He patted his shoulder consolingly, then made his ablutions and entered the dead man's room. His legs began shaking suddenly as he advanced towards the brass bed where his father's body lay. He drew back the end of the sheet covering the face and the flies buzzed, then settled again. Staring at his father's face, he muttered through dry lips:

'Peace be upon you and the mercy of Allah.'

Then he pressed them to the cold forehead. Though incapable of returning the salutation, the dead man had certainly heard him. Crystal tears glinted in his eyes, putting the walls out of focus and setting dancing before his eyes the framed Qur'anic verse in large Kufic calligraphy that stood over the bed:

'Make ready for them such force and tethered horses as you are able – Allah the Great has spoken aright.'

The voices of the sheikhs grew louder as they recited the most beautiful names of Allah. Sheikh Abdul Maqsoud the corpse-washer came forward and drew off the white *galabia* and undid, from round the waist, the black snake-skin belt that the Hagg used to wear, a snake he had shot after it had for long struck terror in Behbesheen.

Sheikh Abdul Maqsoud turned the belt over in his hands, his deep-set eyes gleaming with joy; he then took hold of the dead man's hand and pulled the large gold ring off it: all this had now become his, a contribution of alms made to him by the family in memory of the dead man. He then raised the rigid body with his assistant and laid it down on the wooden plank set over the large brass bowl.

He handed the brass cup to Hassan and advanced the container of pure water towards him, saying:

'Take hold of yourself, my son, otherwise your tears will make the water impure.'

With steady hand Hassan poured the water over the head and body which Sheikh Abdul Maqsoud was rubbing down with soap.

When the voices began reciting the Qur'an they performed the rites of ablution on the dead man, then dried the body. They tore the winding sheets with a shrill screech that jolted Hassan's nerves. He took control of himself as they stitched up the pieces of cloth and wrapped them round the body, tying them securely at the legs and on top of the head. They spread the bed covering in the wooden bier and laid the body on it, then covered it over with the cashmere shawl.

Sheikh Hammad entered and took the brass bedstead to pieces, while the women's voices rose loud with wailing. The brass bedstead had been set up ever since Hagg Aballah's first marriage; Hassan's mother had breathed her last in it, and to it he had brought Muntaha in marriage and in it she had had his other children. But with the death of the master of the house the bedstead must be done away with and not set up again till after the period of mourning.

Hassan gave a sharp cough as the aroma of incense inflamed the sensitivity of his nose and the tears flowed copiously from his eyes. Stolidly, he passed the handkerchief over his face and went forward to take up one of the front shafts of the bier with Sheikh Hammad, who took the other, the rear ones being taken by two faithful retainers. Resting it on their shoulders, they went out into the courtyard.

Owais, the man in charge of the livestock, threw a young water-buffalo to the ground in front of the bier and ran Hamid the butcher's knife over its throat and the blood spilt out on the hot, burning sands in a sacrifice to the dead man.

The men trod across the pool of blood as they bore the bier to the other side of the stone wall and the funeral cortège arranged itself in ranks behind them.

They hurried along with the bier as they fervently uttered, in hoarse voices, the formula of the unity of Allah: there is no god but Allah. The women hastened behind them, clad in the *shagga* that hung down over their bodies like a tent, allowing nothing to show but the gleam of their eyes.

The sun had passed the centre point in the sky but still sent down its searing rays into the sands so that its heat penetrated stingingly through their sandals.

They passed along the winding village lanes till they came down to where the only mosque stood, in the middle of the road that led to the other hill where the ruins of graves lay in ranks at the foot of the mountain.

Casting off their sandals, they took the dead man in and placed him in the *mihrab*. Seven times they uttered the words 'Allah is greatest', then said the funeral prayers, after which they again took up the bier and hurried along with it to the cemetery. The gravedigger had prepared the grave, opening the mouth and removing the earth from the entrance and collecting up the bones of the former inhabitants and tying them up in their decaying shrouds and placing them against the inner wall painted with lime; then he scattered the soft sand mixed with henna, in preparation for laying down the new corpse.

The coffin grew heavier on its bearers as they hurried along, panting hard, their shoulders almost twisted from their bodies; it was as though the dead man was resisting the grave in terror, so that, as they advanced, the front of the bier turned them in the direction of the houses and they progressed with sideways steps. The stalks of maize in the basins of cultivated land gave out, behind red sparks discharged from the sharp blade of the sun, a white vapour that made their eyes smart. Having reached the opening, they put down the bier in front of it.

Sheikh Hammad placed a small pair of scissors in Hassan's hand, saying between his teeth:

'Come along, man, do your duty. Snip the shroud or it will be stolen by those dirty thieves of gravediggers. I swear by the Almighty if one of them falls into my hands I'll hang him on the tree alongside the mosque.'

Then he spat on the ground to show his disgust.

Hassan took the scissors and went down behind the corpse into the darkness of the grave.

The sound of the Qur'an reciters grew louder, speeding up their recitation, as though they had another appointment.

A lizard passed between his feet, then disappeared into the darkness. He squatted down on his knees alongside his father and stretched out his hand with the scissors and began cutting the shroud, careful not to touch the dead flesh. The gravedigger patted him on the shoulder as he muttered:

'Come along, man – may the Lord give him protection.'

He got to his feet and walked backwards behind him, as he gave his salutations to the dead man and then came out into the sunlight. He stood amongst the men till the gravedigger had completed his task and had piled the earth against the entrance and poured water over it, then watered the nearby cactus with what was left.

The sun was now suspended over the peak of the mountain, and it cast forth red shafts of light that made long shadows, depicting vague spectres. The tombs looked similar to the scattered houses in the dusky light of sunset.

Someone called out:

'Say that Allah is One!'

In a deep voice they all muttered fervently:

'There is no god but Allah.'

'Everyone thereon passes away,' quoted the gravedigger, 'and there remains your Lord's face possessed of majesty and splendour.'

'That which Allah has said is the truth,' they all called out.

Stealthily Hassan passed some money to the gravedigger and set about returning, with the crowd following him, to the courtyard of the house.

The men seated themselves on the cane chairs that had been set out in rows with the kerosene lamps above their heads; each time the Qur'an reciter finished a chapter, cups of coffee were handed round. They would listen fervently, rocking to the rhythm, until the reciter concluded by reciting the Fatiha. By this time it was midnight, and the men spread out the palms of their hands, then passed them over their faces in supplication.

Giving Hassan a sideways look, Sheikh Hammad said 'May Allah have mercy upon him, he was a loving father to everybody, and the greatest horseman in the whole district.'

Faraghalli answered him:

'There are plenty of horsemen about, man. What was special about him was that he could put his ear to the ground and say "So-and-so's going along such-and-such a track and he'll be arriving after such-and-such a time" and his words would ring true as a gold guinea.'

Hassan lowered his head in silence. Perhaps these men knew his father better than he did. Was it in fact he himself who was responsible for the estrangement between himself and his father? He took out a wad of notes from his pocket and thrust them into Sheikh Hammad's hand.

'Spend them on what's required – tonight's at my expense.'

Confused by Hassan's generosity, Sheikh Hammad exclaimed:

'What nobility – May the Lord bless you.'

Trays with bowls of broth ranged round with pieces of boiled meat were set up on the low tables, and Hassan rose to invite the men, while he himself ate a little with difficulty, waiting till everyone had dispersed and the pressure lamps had been put out.

Entering the house, he walked in loneliness through its rooms, passing among the women squatting on the mats, clad in black. From the ground there rose a black tent that moved towards him; from two tiny slits there looked out at him two eyes which he

recognized as those of Muntaha, his father's wife. She held out her
hand with a key, muttering in a voice choked by weeping:

'The Hagg Aballah handed over to me the key of the cupboard
in trust for me to give to you.'

'Be strong,' he muttered, taking the key from her.

'Strength is with Allah.'

He went to the cupboard he had known since childhood. As he
did so his eyes fell for an instant on the glistening water on the
floor, left over after the dead man had been washed.

His hand came across a large bundle of notes, also a piece of
paper on which was recorded the names of those who were to
benefit from the sum of money. His gaze came to rest on the name
of his daughter Jasmine mentioned among those to inherit. The
words became blurred and he sat down on the edge of the mattress
that had been laid out on the ground for him to sleep on instead of
the bed that had been dismantled and some of whose pieces were
leaning in the corner against the wall. He placed his head between
his hands and the papers between his outstretched legs. The smell
of the jasmine whose flowers were opening in the night like white
stars was wafted in to him by the breeze. He had said 'Call her
Jasmine.' He had loved her and had mentioned her among his own
children in his will. He had no doubt thought about her and had
perhaps sometimes longed to see her. Why had he not asked to
meet her? More than once he'd said to Louga Hanem, before the
final break: 'We must take a train to the country so my father can
see my child.' She would put her elegant nose in the air and he
would keep silent. Too often he kept silent. Once, during one of the
rare times they met, his father had said:

'Next year, my son, we'll make the pilgrimage together,' and he
had burst into childish laughter.

The years had passed and a life had come to an end and the wish
had not been fulfilled. He smiled sadly at the memory, beset by a
feeling of bafflement. The days had robbed the two of them and
they had not gone. They hadn't even seen enough of each other,
and a sensation of yearning for his father exploded suddenly in his

breast. Which of them was to blame?

He woke up from his thoughts to the echoing howling of the mountain wolves. Had the grave robber done it? Had he left the opening of the grave unclosed after him?

The blood rose up into his neck, as he choked with grief and anger and he let his body fall back as though struck by a blow from the Hagg's famous staff. He had never in fact suffered it. When he was young it was enough for Hagg Aballah to wave it in his face and shout 'The rod's for the insubordinate,' for his weak body to tremble under the imaginary blows.

'Father, you gave me a real beating tonight.'

The winds whistled forlornly through the branches of the date palms, then silence reigned while the jasmine buds carefully folded themselves against the rapidly spreading rays of the sun. The cooing of pigeons rose from the dove-cotes on top of the houses.

Sheikh Hammad's voice called from outside:

'Mr Hassan, the commissioner has sent the jeep to take you to the station – there's half an hour till the train goes.'

Awwad entered carrying the basin and ewer, and in his wake Muntaha, her hair dishevelled and in her nightgown, carrying a tray of breakfast.

He went out to the car. As he got into it he waved at the men who had gathered, then it moved off, leaving behind it a whirlpool of dust that enveloped the children who had risen from sleep and collected at the sound of the car and were now trying to catch up as, with the ends of their *galabias* in their teeth, they ran along on their thin brown legs.

The Flat in Nakshabandi Street

~~~~~~

Aziza woke from the nap she usually took in the heat of the afternoon after a heavy lunch. She got up onto her knees on the Turkish-style sofa that stood under the window, cursing and swearing. With a single thrust she opened the shutters and, hanging half out of the window, screamed at the boys playing football below her. Absorbed in their game, they ran out into the street and a passing car suddenly braked and the driver blew his horn, drowning her voice. Mahmoud was woken by the clamour and rushed out of his room, still in his vest and pyjama trousers. He patted her on the shoulder as she was about to engage in a battle of words with one of her neighbours who was leaning out of her window and watching her son at play. He passed his hand over the sweat that was running down between the hairs on his chest. Immediately she closed the two halves of the glass and sat back:

'God's name protect you, dear – be careful you don't catch cold. Hateful children who don't have any consideration for anyone around. Heaven knows what they'll grow up like.'

'Don't upset yourself, Auntie. The world's not what it was. Look at young Sameh and what he's up to ever since his father bought him a car, coming and going with his hand on the hooter till the doorman opens the garage door for him. Thinks he's become a Bey and is too grand to get out and open it himself.'

She was pleased to find him in agreement with her opinions and the frown went from her face.

'Calm down and make us our afternoon cup of coffee, may the good Lord keep you safe and sound.'

'It's lack of upbringing – not like in our day. Waheeba girl!'

She called and clapped her hands for the servant, then clapped louder and screamed:

'Girl, Waheeba. Where are you hiding yourself? Girl, that's enough sleep for now, go and bring the coffee things. My dear, the girl's for ever chewing away at onions with every meal and so she no sooner sits down than she drops off to sleep like an animal.'

The frown again wrinkled her sallow skin as she drew together her eyebrows pencilled in the form of two high arches above her narrow eyes, lending to her lined face an expression of permanent wrathful indignation. Waheeba, who had joined Aziza's service twenty-five years ago as a child from the village, came stomping along in her filthy peasant *galabia*, with her ungainly body and round, good-humoured face; she was carrying a kitchen tray on which were a spirit lamp, tins of sugar and coffee, and a large *kanaka*[1] filled with water. She placed the tray on the folding iron table, which she drew up close to the edge of the sofa in front of her mistress. Mahmoud took the top off the spirit lamp and lit it with a match which he waved about in the still air till it went out. Waheeba went out and returned with a bright metal tray on which were two cups and a glass of iced water; this she placed on the table alongside the other. As she watched the coffee over the spirit lamp Aziza said:

'Have you washed the entrance hall, girl?'

'But it's clean. Does it have to be washed every single day?'

'Look, my dear, the way the girl answers me back. Girl, I've told you it's for keeping the flat cool. And why are the cups wet? Don't you yet know after all these years how to dry a coffee cup? You're worse than useless. Go and bring a cloth and dry them properly.'

Aziza had nothing to do all day but give orders to Waheeba from where she sat on the sofa and amuse herself with looking out of the window till she went off to her bed in the small bedroom at the back of the flat. The view from the window revealed the whole of Nakshabandi Street right up to the intersection with Mumtaz Street. Directly facing the flat lay the house of Sheikh Wagdi and his family, surrounded by a garden; it was one of the few old houses that had not been divided up into flats or pulled down to make way for a large block. Between Sheikh Wagdi's house and the top of the street were various shops whose activity was a source of interest to Aziza: Bayoumi's shop from which he sold sugar-cane juice, an ironing establishment, and a grocery; then there was the 'Paris Salon', a ladies' coiffeur. On her own side of the street – and out of view unless she craned out of the window – was a large block of flats which provided the street with the boys who had turned it into a football pitch and who were under constant verbal attack from Aziza.

Though she was known as Mrs Aziza, she was in fact a spinster and was now approaching seventy. She used to live with her brother Saleh and her sister Zeinab after their father had died, her mother having died when they were young children and their father not having remarried. He had been a cotton broker living in Benha and used to travel among the towns of the Delta. He had been able to put aside a certain amount of money more through thrift than any particular business flare. Then Zeinab, though the younger, had married and moved to Cairo with her husband, and Aziza had stayed on with Saleh in the family house in Benha. Saleh had then been offered a job with prospects in a cigarette company in Cairo, so he had sold the house in Benha, dividing the proceeds amongst the three of them, and had rented a flat near Bab el-Louk station, taking Aziza and Waheeba with him, so that they might be near Zeinab, who had settled into the Nakshabandi Street flat in the district of Abdin, where she had given birth to her son Mahmoud.

Saleh, on reaching a position in the company which would allow him to marry and at the same time to give Aziza a sufficient allowance for her to continue in the flat, had become set in his bachelor ways; besides which he had been having an affair with the Greek wife of one of his colleagues, who turned a blind eye to his wife's behaviour. Aziza, on her part, found the arrangement convenient and would tell herself, and others, that she had sacrificed herself to looking after her brother. In fact, though, her state of spinsterhood was not so much a matter of sacrifice or preference as due to her not being possessed of any great beauty, her nose being unnaturally large for her pinched face, and her body lacking that rounded softness that attracts men. Also, it was only much later in life, with the death of Saleh, that she had inherited the savings bonds he had been buying in her name and which would have been an inducement for a prospective husband. Shortly after Saleh's death Zeinab and her husband had been killed in a car crash and it was natural that Aziza should move into the Nakshabandi Street flat, together with Waheeba, in order to look after Mahmoud. On Saleh's death Aziza had taken to wearing black as though she had been widowed, though she still continued to dye her hair with black Baghdadi henna. In Mahmoud, so like his uncle in his looks and ways, she had found a substitute for Saleh.

Since taking up residence in Nakshabandi Street she would spend her days sitting on the sofa and watching the neighbours and the passers-by. Each morning she would ask Mahmoud at breakfast to read out the page in the newspaper listing those who had died. Whenever she heard a name she knew, however remotely, she would spring into action and put a long black overcoat on top of her house *galabia*, taking under her arm her leather handbag in which she kept a handkerchief with a black lace border. She would go off with Mahmoud, who would take her and leave her at the deceased's house. From the moment she entered she would without dispute occupy the place of honour in the gathering by reason of the laments and dirges she knew by heart that befitted every possible circumstance. Holding her handkerchief with its black lace border, she would jerk it about with both hands from side to side to the beat of her rhyming words and the ladies present would burst into loud screams and wailing. She would fix them with a stare that was as cruel as that of death and would dab at her eyes with her handkerchief between the verses as though she were crying. When the mourning ceremony was over she would wait for Mahmoud, who, having finished his work at the girls' school, would pass by and take her home. These were the only occasions on which she allowed herself to pass beyond the front door of the flat. Apart from this the only other activity she indulged in was the cooking. Once a day she would enter the kitchen and seat herself on a low wooden stool and Waheeba would bring her the primus stove already lit and all the various pots and pans she required, handing them to her as she demanded them. As they worked together she would curse and swear at Waheeba from time to time and sometimes Waheeba would mumble back in protest, but her words would be lost against the hissing of the primus. Having finished the cooking, Aziza would return to her place on the sofa under the window. And so this routine of life had continued for the last fifteen years in this flat and Mahmoud was now in his early thirties, having graduated and taken a post as a teacher of French in a girls' school.

The coffee came to the boil and Aziza poured it into the two cups, leaving a little for Waheeba in the *kanaka*. Waheeba took up the tray and went with it to the kitchen where she added more water, coffee and sugar and made herself a generous brew.

Mahmoud took up his cup and began sipping at it as he looked sideways at his aunt, waiting for the right time to speak. Suddenly Aziza gave a yell and opened the window:

'Run, girl, and catch the cucumber man.'

Mahmoud stretched out his neck, and said:

'Auntie, the man's calling out "Beans, fine beans".'

'Really? I quite thought he was saying "Lovely cucumbers".'

She went back to sipping her coffee. Mahmoud gave a little cough, then, looking down into his cup, said:

'I say, Auntie, what do you think about my giving private lessons to some of the students during the last month before the exams?'

She tightened her eyebrows and her nose hung down till it

93

touched the rim of the cup. She took a sip, and then said:

'My dear boy, don't do anything so ridiculous. What'll people say when they find I'm sitting here with girls coming and going through our flat?'

'Auntie, they're only young girls, not as old as my children would be had I married early.'

'Eh? What's that you're saying?'

As she said these words she held her fingers to her ear. Mahmoud wondered whether she really didn't hear well or just didn't hear what she didn't want to hear. His reverie was broken by the sound of his aunt savouring the coffee in her mouth.

'My dear boy, why should you trouble yourself with stupid girls who fail their exams? Any of them who really wants to study can do so on her own. It's not as if we need the money.'

'Auntie, it's not a question of money. The whole point of the thing is how to occupy oneself in something useful instead of sitting at the café.'

'What a shame, my dear boy – begrudging yourself sitting about with your friends and enjoying yourself with a couple of games of backgammon.'

He sat on, staring into his cup, then took a final sip.

'You're right, Auntie. If you'll excuse me now.'

He rose to his feet and went to his room where he stretched out on the bed. Putting his hand under the pillow, he brought out a packet of cigarettes and a lighter. He lit a cigarette and thought what a miserable life it was when he couldn't smoke in her presence, especially as coffee wasn't really the same without a cigarette to go with it, and that if he tried to do so he'd get a long lecture about the harm smoking did and what a waste of money it was. He thought with regret that he wasn't even able to give girls private lessons. You never knew – girls grew up quickly these days and many was the story he'd heard about their goings-on. He gazed at the cloud of smoke above him and thought how enjoyable it would be if he were able to make the acquaintance of one of his students' older sisters, a modern girl who went out to work and had her own flat, instead of creeping along at night to the kitchen where Waheeba slept. He was always afraid his aunt would come to know, though at the same time he doubted whether she hadn't yet noticed something after all these years, especially as Waheeba sometimes found pleasure in arousing Aziza's suspicions. Wasn't it strange, though, that she had never spoken to him about this matter? In any event, what harm did it do Waheeba who after all had been married once in the days when she was with his uncle and aunt and had then divorced and returned to work for them? He awoke from his dreams to feel the cigarette burning his fingers. He threw it from the open window, then got up and washed his face and dressed. He poured eau-de-Cologne into the palms of his hands and passed them over his chin and cheeks as he stared at himself with approval in the mirror, though he would have wished for his nose to be like his father's rather than it being one of the features inherited from his mother's side. As he passed through to the front door he saw that his aunt was looking out of the window.

'Goodbye, Auntie. Anything you want me to bring?'

'Bring a water-melon with you, because that useless wretch of a woman always buys rotten ones. What do you feel like having for lunch tomorrow?'

'Anything, anything made by you is delicious.'

He shut the door behind him and she thought: would it be better to do some okra in the oven or make stuffed eggplant? Then she turned to the window as she heard two boys squabbling in the street.

'Get out of here, the pair of you,' she screamed, leaning out of the window. 'May the dog-catcher take you off in his cart.'

She waited till Mahmoud appeared from the door of the building and shouted: 'Hit them, Mahmoud – they need to be given a lesson, those two.'

On seeing Mahmoud the two boys ran away. He walked along till he turned off left into Mumtaz Street and went to the Safeer Café where his friends were waiting for him. Directly he had disappeared from Nakshabandi Street Waheeba came and stood behind her mistress, standing on tiptoe so that she could make out the whole street. She knew that Aziza didn't like her to take such liberties in Mahmoud's presence. The two of them watched Bayoumi, the seller of sugar-cane juice, as he drove the flies away from his shop with a fly-whisk, slumped in a chair in front of the marble counter. Beside him he had a small transistor radio and was singing in accompaniment with Umm Kulthum.[2]

'Look, look,' said Waheeba, pointing to the end of the street. 'It's the gentleman with the red rose, owner of the Paris Salon, passing by and he's looking up at our window as usual. Really, I don't know why you don't marry him.'

'Girl, don't be so daft – do you think I'd look at a hairdresser? Every day he passes by and I don't pay him any attention. I know he comes by this way because of me. What shall I do though, one can't command one's heart. Also, it's not as if I'm short of anything that I've got to say "All right, let's just get married." Or maybe you've forgotten the disaster of your own marriage.'

'All the same, lady, it's the customary thing and wealth and children are the ornament of this world.'

'Whatever next, girl? – and you even know how to quote the Qur'an.'

As the call to the evening prayers sounded the street lights came on. The grocer left his shop and spread several mats on the pavement in the direction of the qiblah[3], while Sheikh Wagdi came down from his house with his son Sameh behind him, and the men appeared and formed up in rows behind the Sheikh, together with the grocer, and began performing their prayers. Aziza contented herself with looking at them from where she sat. She had prayed a lot during her lifetime and had then told herself one day that she had not committed sins like other women and that she was continually doing good by attending funeral ceremonies and comforting people in times of adversity and that she was thus entitled to reward from the Almighty. The idea pleased her that she no longer prayed, though she always enjoyed watching Sheikh Wagdi leading the men in prayer. When the men had finished their prayers and had dispersed, the young boys returned to take up their game once aain.

Dr Farid came down and went on his way to the café. A little later his wife Amina appeared and walked quickly in the opposite direction.

'Do you see what I see, lady? She's wearing her daughter's red dress and is done up to the nines.'

'Eh?' said Aziza, placing her fingers round her ear. 'Someone's come to ask for her daughter in marriage?'

'Marriage? Who'll ever marry her daughter with her mother's reputation stinking the place out? I was saying that she was wearing her daughter's dress.'

'Oh, I know that. What I'd like is for you to follow her and find out where she goes to, but you're so clumsy she'd see you and be put off.'

'And why should I follow her? We all know what she's up to. Give me the money and let me be off to buy the vegetables.'

'Ah, girl, that's all you're good at. I'd really like to know where you disappear to for all that time. Woman, the greengrocer's right at the corner of the street.'

'Not again! I've told you his vegetables are all dried up and past their best and I get them cheaper from Nasiriyya. D'you think I enjoy walking all that way?'

'Heavens, girl, why do you answer me back like that? If you don't mind that tongue of yours I'll get Mahmoud to give you a good hiding.'

'I swear it's only because he's so nice I stay on. He's good and kind. Give me the money and let me be off.'

Aziza put her hand inside the front of her *galabia* and took out her purse. She searched through the bundle of notes and handed over the most ancient one she could find. Waheeba took the pound note from her as though handling a dead rat by the tail.

'Buy some eggplant for stuffing and all the bits and pieces and come straight back.'

'All right.'

Waheeba went into the kitchen and put on her clean *galabia* for going out in, which was hanging on the nail fixed to the kitchen door, and took up the shopping bag. As she was opening the front door Aziza turned to her:

'Put on the night light above the door and don't be late.'

Waheeba put on the blue lamp that cast a dim light over the entrance, leaving the rest of the flat immersed in darkness. For Waheeba this was her real day, beginning from the moment she went out to the market. It was for this that she put up with things as she did. She would go to the Nasiriyya *souk* where she would meet up with her friends, servants and shopkeepers who would receive her with warmth and affection. They would give her tea and she would enjoy recounting what went on in the house in her own particular way that was at variance with what actually happened. Sometimes she would even make up incidents that showed her as having the upper hand in the house.

Aziza went back to looking out of the window. In the west the sky was turning an orange colour; across it a silvery aeroplane moved slowly towards the airport, a red light flashing on and off. Suddenly she became aware that the melon seed and peanut vendor had stopped with his cart in front of the building. He raised his head towards the window.

'A very good evening to you, lady.'

'Give me five piastres' worth of melon seeds and five of peanuts.'

'Certainly.'

Once again she brought out her purse and took a ten piastre piece from it. She placed it in the basket attached by a rope to a nail fixed to the window-sill and carefully let it down the three storeys till it was in the vendor's hands. He took the money and put two paper cones into the basket and looked up at her. She drew the basket up and placed it in the corner, then opened the cone of melon seeds and began splitting them open and spitting the husks out of the window. She thought about Waheeba at the Nasiriyya *souk* and where she spent all this long time away, returning only after the evening prayer. Of course she used to steal from the money she was given; all servants did. Whenever she told Mahmoud this he would laugh and she would say to him that it was no laughing matter because he himself had made that money with the sweat of his brow.

She threw the empty paper cones from the window and looked up at the dark sky and the scattered stars. With the call to evening prayers the shopkeepers let down the shutters and fixed locks on them. The men lined up for prayer and the boys dispersed to their homes.

She remembered the letter she had received that morning from the bank. She savoured, like food, the thought of time going by and the money in the bank increasing, for the bank automatically reinvested the interest in further savings bonds. By being careful and keeping an eye on things, especially on Waheeba, they were able to live on Mahmoud's salary. He would hand it over to her the first of every month and, though she knew that he kept back an amount for his cigarettes, she would give him ten pounds a month pocket money. The letter from the bank informed her that her fortune had amounted to a total of over fifty-four thousand pounds. As often happened previously when she received the bank's statement she found herself asking: should she tell Mahmoud of the amount and surprise him with its largeness or leave him in ignorance? After due consideration she decided that it was wiser to leave him guessing as to the amount he would be inheriting from her.

Her thoughts led her to consider the relationship between Mahmoud and Waheeba and what occurred between them from time to time at night in the kitchen. The temptation to let him know that she was aware of these goings-on was great, but she realized that – as with the amount of money in the bank – her strength lay in retaining these two cards in her hand. She thought, too, of the post office savings book in which Mahmoud would place Waheeba's monthly wages. Once a month she would show Waheeba that the payment had been made and would then lock the book away in her wardrobe. Every now and again Waheeba would lose her temper and rebel and demand her money so that she could take herself off to her village as she had done once many years ago. Aziza would agree and explain to her that Mahmoud would have to go to the post office and withdraw the money, and in the meantime she would remind her of how hard life was in the countryside and Waheeba would calm down and agree to stay on.

Stillness reigned in the street. The widely separated street lamps threw pale blotches of light onto the pavement. Directly ahead, shafts of light slipped through shutters in Sheikh Wagdi's house, drawing lines that showed up the greenness of the grass under the window. In the far corners of the garden the mango trees stood out, huge and shapeless, against the lesser darkness. This stillness and darkness brought about in Aziza a deep melancholy after her busy day, an acute sensation that her life somehow contained no future. Everyone else lived in hope yet her own life was a struggle to ensure that the present routine continued for ever.

A sharp pain in the chest caused her to release her grip on the window-sill and she fell back on the sofa. Immediately she regretted having eaten so much at lunch, then realized with paralyzing terror that the pain was not a mere attack of indigestion and that she should not move till Mahmoud or Waheeba returned and could call the doctor. She remained lying cocooned in her pain, staring up towards the window. In the vast sky thousands of stars looked down at her, winking. She tried in vain to struggle against the giddiness that swept her up, weightless and without control, into that overhanging vault, and soon there was nothing but her pain and her terror binding her to her sofa in the flat in Nakshabandi Street.

Notes

1. Metal pot in which Turkish coffee is made.
2. The most famous Arab woman singer of this century, who died in 1975.
3. The direction of the Kaaba in Mecca towards which Muslims turn in praying.

Degrees of Death

One day my grandmother said to me:

'We've bought you some rabbits.'

I stared at her blankly: I wasn't quite sure what she meant.

'Didn't you always say you'd like to have rabbits? Well, we've bought you a pair, one male and one female.'

'So they'll have babies,' I said, showing off some of the knowledge in these matters I had recently acquired.

'God willing,' said my grandmother with a smile. At that moment Nanny Zareefa came along with grandmother's second cup of coffee of the day and she began rolling yet another cigarette, her misshapen fingers trembling as they attempted to spread the tobacco evenly along the slip of paper. Disliking the smell of the tobacco and the smoke that made my eyes water, I jumped up from her side and ran out.

I wandered round the garden and eventually found Hasan watering the vegetable patch at the back of the house.

'The rabbits?' I asked. 'Where are the rabbits?'

Taking up the hose, he walked back to the tap and turned off the water. He then took me by the hand – his own as rough as the loofah they used for washing my back and which always made me feel that a whole layer of skin had been peeled off me. We passed the chicken house, the dirty pool where a few ducks waddled in and out of the water, till we came to the large mud pigeon cote, glaring white in the summer sun, standing on its wooden supports, with the frail ladder leaning against one of them. To one side stood a large cardbord box over the front of which had been fixed a piece of wire netting.

I squatted down and looked into the darkness. All I could see was a single pair of golden eyes staring out at me.

'Is there only one?' I asked in disappointment.

'No, there are two,' said Hasan. 'It's difficult to see them. I'll bring them out one by one. We don't want them to escape, do we?'

He cautiously lifted up the wire netting from the bottom and inserted his hand. A few seconds later it came out followed by a struggling bundle of fur grasped by a hind leg.

'Do they bite?' I asked.

Hasan laughed and set the small body into the palm of his other hand. 'Put your hands together,' he said. Fearfully I cupped my hands and he placed the rabbit in them. The intense warmth of the body, the softness of the fur, and the trembling that racked its whole frame sent a wave of pity and yearning through me. I stood looking down at its brown, hunched up body in wonder.

Hasan brought out the other struggling rabbit and held it up in front of me by its ears. I protested but he told me that this was the best way to hold them, that it didn't hurt them at all. This time it was a black one with a white splodge on its face.

'This is the male,' said Hasan. I looked at it again. I decided I preferred the one I was holding.

The following day Hasan made them an enclosure where they could hop about and nibble at the clover I would push through the wire netting at them. Sometimes, with Hasan's help, we'd open the door that was held fast by a clasp and a large stone, and I'd go inside and lie flat on my stomach and watch the two rabbits in their leisurely existence.

I had been brought up in the country surrounded by chickens and ducks and geese, also a donkey that I was sometimes allowed to ride. With none of these had I been able to form any sort of relationship: I had found the chickens silly, the ducks hard to get near, the donkey generally not available, and the geese frightening (though the memory of kind old Nanny Zareefa grasping a goose between her fleshy thighs and force-feeding it remains indelibly imprinted on my mind).

In due time the rabbits had babies and the whole family came to occupy me more and more. The fact that they had fur rather than feathers made them for me utterly different creatures from the various species of poultry. They seemed to me even more delightful than the farm cat which you couldn't pick up without being scratched. Multi-coloured balls of fluff with twitching noses, they would squat almost motionless throughout the long hot days, seeking the shade cast by the struts of wood from which Hasan had made their enclosure, then in the evening hopping about among the heaps of clover.

Then one early morning, as I was running through the courtyard on my way to the fields, I saw Nanny Zareefa bending over something held in her grasp. I tried to call out but the horror of what I was witnessing blocked off any sound. Nanny Zareefa had not seen me; if she had she would surely have spared me the sight of the quick movement of the knife and the blood spurting down the white front of one of the baby rabbits, and her hand holding it to the stone paving as its legs kicked and pumped out a crimson pool.

I rushed back into the house and upstairs to the privacy of my room to mourn the rabbit with silent tears. I blamed myself for not having called out and pleaded with her for its life. It was my first felt encounter with death and it provided me with the bitter knowledge that for grown-ups there were, as it were, degrees of death, one for humans and another for animals. Later in life I was to discover that many of us also think in terms of degrees of death where our fellow men are concerned, but that only very few of us become capable of viewing our own death with equanimity.

The Kite

Rubbing the sleep from her eyes Widad got up from the mattress in the corner of the one room that made up the house and which, during her husband's lifetime, had served for the two of them in addition to their numerous children. Now for some years she had had it to herself and had become accustomed to the silence that reigned over it and the dull routine that was her daily life. She smiled as she heard the cockerels, her own and those of her neighbours, greeting the first light of day and almost drowning the voice of the *muezzin* as he called to dawn prayers.

Her first thoughts were of her chickens that would be waiting for her to let them out of their coop into the courtyard alongside the house. Years ago she had made the coop with her own hands out of mud and reeds, with straw on the floor for them to lay their eggs on. In those days the chickens had helped to provide for the needs of the children, especially as her husband Ahmed's health had been deteriorating and he had been able to do less and less work as an agricultural labourer. Now the chickens were not only her support in life but gave it a flavour and a meaning.

She went to the water-pump that stood in the corner of the courtyard, working it with her left hand and spattering the water over her face and neck with the other. All this while the screeching from the coop grew more and more insistent. 'I'm coming, I'm coming,' she called out. 'Just have a little patience.' She walked across the courtyard and moved aside with her foot the stone that kept the wire-netting door shut and two large cockerels strutted out, followed by the harem of hens over which they were continually fighting. Widad laughed with pleasure and pride as the chickens scattered over the courtyard. She knew each one of them and its particular characteristics and would carry on long conversations with them.

She looked up at the cloudless sky that told of a day of extreme heat. She screwed up her eyes and looked beyond the mud wall that bounded the courtyard towards the dark forms of the tall date-palms and eucalyptus trees marking the river bank beyond the bright green of the fields that stretched to the water's edge. From afar came the painful groaning of a water-wheel being turned by a blindfolded water-buffalo.

She went back into the house and brought out a palm-branch cage; she took it to the courtyard and raised the little door and an army of chicks jostled to get through the narrow opening and join the chickens. Then she took from the coop a heavy earthenware bowl, threw to one side the water that remained and, rinsing it at the pump, refilled it and put it down in a corner of the courtyard where, in an hour or two when the sun had made a part of its journey across the sky, there would be an area of shade. And so, pursuing the strict routine she had set herself these last few years, she went back into the house to prepare the mixture of bran and curdled milk. As she appeared with the full bowl the chickens flocked round her and she scooped up the moist bran in her fingers and threw it down around her. As she scooped the last handful from the bowl she saw with annoyance some of her neighbours' pigeons flutter down amidst her chickens.

Only now did she prepare her own breakfast: a glass of strong, heavily-sugared tea and some pieces of bread and a small bowl of whey. She carried them on a tray and sat down by the coop where she ate and sipped at the tea, deriving a deep-seated sense of security from watching her chickens pecking about in the earth in their never-ending search for things to eat. It was this time at the beginning of the day that she loved most, when man starts his struggle for his daily bread, and the animals and plants join with him in the renewal of God's miracle of creation. She looked around at her small tribe of chickens of which she was in charge and raised her hand to her lips, kissing it back and front in thanks for His generosity.

She regretted that it was only through such gestures and the uttering of a few simple supplications that she was able to render her thanks to her Maker. During Ahmed's lifetime she would stand behind him as he performed the prayers, following his movements as he bowed down and then prostrated himself, listening reverently to the words he recited and knowing that he who stands behind the man leading prayers and follows his movements has himself performed the prayers. Ahmed had often tried to make her memorize some verses of the Qur'an but she had never succeeded in doing so, and thus, with his death, she had given up performing the regular prayers and was too shy to ask one of the neighbours if she could join his family in their prayers.

The voice of the *muezzin* broke the silence as he gave the call to noon prayers. She rose to her feet and said 'Allah is great and to Allah be praise', then called 'kutkutkutkutkut' and the chicks hurried along to her and she collected them up and placed them back in their cage, taking it into the house with her, out of the harsh rays of the midday sun, and sprinkled it with water.

She swept the room, then sat down on the ground and gripped the grinder between her thighs, turning the handle and feeding it grains of maize for her chickens' evening meal. Then she boiled two eggs for herself, which she ate with two rounds of bread and an onion, after which she lay down beside the cage with her arm under her head, and before sleep overcame her she heard the call to afternoon prayers.

She was roused from sleep by the chirping of her chicks, and she took up the cage and went outside. She released them again, assured that the sun's golden disk had now lost its power to damage them and had grown a darker orange colour, preparatory to the blood redness of its daily expiry.

She worked the water-pump and washed the sweat from her face, neck and arms, then raised each foot under the jet of water and returned to the house. She brewed up some tea and placed a glass and the tin of sugar on a tray and took them with her through the courtyard to the door that led to the narrow alleyway passing between the closely-packed houses. There, on the raised stone bench beside her house, she sat down to watch the village life pass by. It was the only time of the day when she was in touch with the outside world: men passing, their hoes resting on their shoulders; women in groups, interrupting their chatter to say a word of greeting to her; some children, playing and chasing after each other, the ends of their *galabias* held between their teeth; and animals being led to the canal to be immersed in its cool waters after the heat of the day.

Suddenly she became aware of a man standing by her. She first saw his splayed, cracked feet, then his large hands with the protuberant veins held at his side, then the broad shoulders from which the *galabia* hung down, and the strong, sharp features that still retained vestiges of that handsomeness that had attracted her to him so many years ago.

'Greetings to you, Widad. I hope you're keeping well.'

'Mitwalli?'

Before he replied she had drawn the end of her head-veil in an automatic gesture over her face. Mitwalli had been her childhood sweetheart, yet though each knew of the feelings of the other they had never once exchanged a word. She had presumed that one day he'd go to her father and ask for her hand. However, her father had married her to Ahmed and she had not dared to object. Later Mitwalli had married Nabawiyya, the daughter of Hagg Kattab. During the years she had borne her children, some of whom had lived and others died, and from time to time she would hear news of Mitwalli: that he had had a second son, or that his daughter had married, or that his father had died and left him nearly a *feddan* of good land. It was in the same year his father had died that her husband Ahmed had succumbed to the bilharzia from which he had been suffering all his life. At the time people whispered among themselves that maybe Mitwalli would take her as a second wife now that she was free, but she had silenced such tongues by announcing that she would not think of marrying again and that she would live the rest of her life bringing up her children; besides, she could not accept the idea of sharing a husband with another woman. Now, some months back, Nabawiyya had died.

She knew at once why he had come and for a moment she felt breathless with excitement. She had thought of this possibility ever since she had learnt of the death of his wife, but she had rejected it, telling herself that she had grown used to living on her own. She lowered her head-veil and looked up at him boldly and it was he who looked away.

'I've been wanting to talk to you for some time, Widad,' he said in a low voice. 'You know, Widad, the fact is . . .'

'Sit down, Mitwalli, and have a glass of tea.'

He seated himself on the edge of the stone bench and she poured him out the tea in her empty glass. She added some sugar and passed him the glass. For some time he went on stirring the tea in silence, then said in the same low voice:

'You know, Widad, that my wife, the mother of my children, died and I'm on my own. And you know I've always loved you and wanted you . . .'

'Ah!' she exclaimed. 'Have some shame, man! Have you come to tell me things you should have said thirty years ago? Why didn't you go to my father at the time? You come talking of love when I've got one foot on the ground and one in the grave?'

He sipped at the tea slowly, shifting his feet as though about to leave.

'And do you think I'm any younger, Widad? I'm still five years older than you like before. It was you I always wanted but it wasn't possible at the time. After all, it's not as if we've got anything to lose. The past is over and done with. Or does it mean that just because we've grown old we've not got the right to live the rest of our lives like other people? Anyway, I'll pass by tomorrow at the same time and you think about it in the meantime.'

Though she shook her head at him, a great sadness took hold of her as she watched those large feet turn away and walk off. She thought with pain of how her life might have been had she married Mitwalli instead of Ahmed, but there is a time for everything: a time for romantic dreams, and a time for marriage and child-bearing, and a time when God has decreed that you are left alone in this world in order to prepare yourself for leaving it.

She took up the tray and stood in the doorway to the courtyard and watched the two cockerels squabbling over the ownership of a worm. Suddenly a kite swooped down by the chicken coop on the far side, then flew off with a chick between its claws. The chickens were momentarily struck motionless by this event, then continued their normal activities as though nothing had happened. As for her, the loss of the chick clouded out every other thought from her mind. What would prevent the kite from coming again?

Hurriedly she gathered up the chickens into the coop and the chicks into their cage.

Sleep did not come to her till far into the night as she tossed and turned and worried about her chickens. Just before sleep finally lay down on her eyelids there came to her the spectre of the tall, gaunt figure of Mitwalli standing in the courtyard with arms outstretched, like a scarecrow protecting her chickens. 'And why not?' she asked herself.

In a short dream before she awoke to the call to dawn prayers she saw herself standing behind Mitwalli and following his movements as he prayed, and her heart stirred with a feeling of contentment.

Just Another Day

〰〰〰〰〰〰〰〰〰〰〰〰〰〰〰〰〰〰〰〰〰〰〰〰〰
. . . .

As always I woke up in a state of heavy lethargy. I wake each dawn to the sound of the *muezzin*'s call to prayers, make my prayers, then go back to bed and sleep late. Today I enjoyed lying there in bed and not getting up. I was tired, tired and weary. What did it matter if I were to stay on as I was? The idea appealed to me and I stretched out my legs to the corners of the bed and closed my eyes. The children had gone out early to their work and had left my breakfast ready on the table in the dining room so that all I had to do was boil up a kettle for tea. But what was the point? I wasn't hungry. What was to stop me staying on in bed? I had grown tired of pretending I had jobs to do that filled my day, while in actual fact I had no role to fulfil. This state of affairs had been going on for a long time, ever since I had grown old and my children had grown up. Even so, I would get up each day, wash my face and comb my hair and, putting on a dressing-gown, would have my breakfast, then go back to my bedroom and dress to go out.

I'd walk to the market and stand in the queues at the shops and cooperatives. I would meet the same faces day after day, and generally I would get into conversation with one of the women as we stood awaiting our turn. We'd always talk about the ever-increasing rise in prices and where would it all end, and we'd exchange a few words about the good old days. Sometimes, when it came to my turn, I would forget what it was I wanted to buy, so I'd get some more sugar or rice, which always come in handy.

Sometimes I'd find some poor exhausted woman, perhaps carrying her child, and I'd give up my place to her, for time no longer mattered to me. I'd noticed that people didn't have the manners of long ago and that they'd push and try to break into the queue. Many a time I'd tell them that the country wouldn't progress if each of us didn't have some manners and proper behaviour. Although they would laugh at my words, they'd make themselves into proper queues, though I'm sure, directly my back was turned, they'd return to their pushing and shoving. On occasions Ali, the man serving at the cooperative, would tell me that the sugar, for instance, hadn't yet come in but that if I liked to come back after an hour or two he'd keep me a kilo, and this would give me the excuse to come out again. Then, when we were at lunch, I'd tell the children how Ali had saved some sugar for me and I'd had to go back to get it, and the children would say: 'Bravo, Mummy. Sugar's like gold dust these days. Ali must have a soft spot for you.'

Approximately once every month I'd go down to the centre of the city. The children would hire me a taxi and they'd arrange that he'd call for me at, say, ten and take me from where we lived in Heliopolis and drop me off at places like Le Salon Vert or Seidnawi's in Kasr el-Nil and would pick me up again at one and take me back in time for lunch. The children would give me a great welcome back and would examine my purchases: a scarf perhaps, or bedroom slippers or something of the sort, though the drawers were already full of such things that I hadn't yet worn. Buying things had become a way of eating up time.

When I was young I'd take my children to play in the park, where I'd see groups of old women sitting on the wooden benches under the trees. They would chatter away amongst themselves, sometimes all of them talking at once. Some of them knitted as they talked or watched the children playing. I used to tell myself that one day I would spend my time like them. But it seems there aren't any more parks in Cairo. The children and the elderly are not catered for in a city that is unable even to provide its citizens with homes because of the way they are increasing so rapidly.

During the last few years, as I get older, I notice myself spending more time in bringing to mind past memories, especially during the short period between waking up and getting out of bed. Sometimes I remember incidents from way back that I'd completely forgotten. It seems that, although every single moment of one's life is stored away in the depths of one's mind, it is the happy moments that lie nearest the surface and are most easily recalled. No wonder old people like to live in the past.

Today, I told myself, I'd stay on in bed. What was the point of getting up?

Faint street noises crept in through the shutters: passing vendors calling their wares, the faraway hooting of traffic, and the dulled sounds of men at work on a nearby building site.

I saw myself as a little girl, standing with Abduh the gardener in my father's country house at Inchass. The sun had just gone down after a scorching summer's day and Abduh, his *galabia* hitched up, was watering the garden. He was holding the hose and pressing his thumb over the end of it so that the water spurted out in arcs of sparkling spray into a cluster of lime trees, removing the dust from the leaves so that they breathed with renewed life. Then he handed me the hose and I moved to a flower bed alongside the steps that led up to the front door of the house. I let the water fall onto the parched, cracked earth, and its dusty surface turned into a dark black mud. As the mud sucked up the water it gave out a heavy green aroma.

The scene was not disturbed by my daugher suddenly coming in and standing at my bedside and saying 'Hullo, Mummy, having a nice rest in bed?' I had no desire to reply or even to open my eyes. My only wish was to retain the image of the water striking against the earth in their eternal mating. Some time later my daughter came back with my son. They stood in the doorway. I thought that perhaps she was annoyed because I hadn't replied to her, so I muttered a few conciliatory words, but I don't believe she heard them. They closed the door behind them.

Later on I thought I heard my brother's voice. He hadn't paid me a visit for ages because his wife and I don't get on. Then I heard her unmistakable shrilly raucous voice. I called out at the top of my voice asking them to keep quiet, that I wanted to rest.

Suddenly the door of the bedroom opened and a woman I hadn't seen before entered. She began undressing me and when I tried to resist I discovered I was quite unable to move. The sounds from the next room were drowned by the monotonous voice of a Qur'an reciter. He was reciting the final verses of the Chapter of the Dawn. When he repeated the words 'And enter My Garden', a feeling of peace flowed over me and I abandoned myself to the hands of the woman.

THE AFRICAN WRITERS SERIES

The book you have been reading is part of Heinemann's long-established series of African fiction. Details of some of the other titles available in this series are given below, but for a catalogue giving information on all the titles available in this series and in the Caribbean Writers Series write to:
Heinemann Educational Publishers,
Halley Court, Jordan Hill, Oxford OX2 8EJ;
United States customers should write to:
Heinemann, 361 Hanover Street,
Portsmouth, NH 03801-3912, USA

SYL CHENEY-COKER
The Last Harmattan of Alusine Dunbar

The first novel of this well-known poet tells the story of a Sierra Leone-like country and its pioneers seeking freedom after the American Revolution.

NADINE GORDIMER
Crimes of Conscience

A selection of short stories which vividly describe human conditions and the turmoil of a violent world outside the individual incidents, where the instability of fear and uncertainty lead unwittingly to crimes of conscience

NGŨGĨ
Matigari

This is a moral fable telling the story of a freedom fighter and his quest for Truth and Justice. Set in the political dawn of post-independence Kenya.
'Clear, subtle, mischievous passionate novel'. *Sunday Times*

AMECHI AKWANYA
Orimili

Set in a complex Nigerian Community that's at the point of irrevocable change, this is the story of a man's struggle to be accepted in the company of his town's elders.

SHIMMER CHINODYA
Harvest of Thorns

'Zimbabwe has fine black writers and Shimmer Chinodya is one of the best. *Harvest of Thorns* brilliantly pictures the transition between the old, white-dominated Southern Rhodesia, through the Bush War, to the new black regime. It is a brave book, a good strong story, and it is often very funny. People who know the country will salute its honesty, but I hope newcomers to African writing will give this book a try. They won't be disappointed.'
Doris Lessing

CHINUA ACHEBE
Things Fall Apart

This, the first title in the African Writers Series, describes how a man in the Igbo tribe of Nigeria became exiled from the tribe and returned only to be forced to commit suicide to escape the results of his rash courage against the white man.